Praise for *Casting Lots*

"I have been waiting for this boo
Elisheva Nesher's presentations
ern Jews and others interested
assumed divination was outlawed or even unknown in ancient
times. Elisheva does not just present the system of using the
aleph-beit to cast lots for spiritual guidance and wisdom, she
also shows the range of divine beings and spiritual practices in
ancient Canaan and Israel, as well as in the modern polytheist revival. There is a warmth and generosity here towards all
sides that we all can learn from."

—Rachel Pollack, author of *Seventy-Eight Degrees of Wisdom*
and *A Walk Through the Forest of Souls*

"In *Casting Lots*, Elisheva Nesher not only clearly details the
history and current practice of Hebrew lot casting but also
offers a rare glimpse into a nonrabbinic earth-based approach
to Jewish spirituality or, as she might prefer, Ivrit or Hebrew
spirituality. Elisheva sharing her wisdom on lot casting would
have been enough (dayenu!), but her sharing of AMHA with
a wider world is a gift. This book will be a valuable resource
to anyone interested in spiritually working with the Hebrew
letters, different approaches to divination, magickal ethics,
Jewish magick and Jew-ish earth-based spirituality."

—Kohenet Ketzirah haMa'agelet,
founder of Devotaj Sacred Arts

"A beautiful and inspiring book, *Casting Lots* by Elisheva Nesher presents a very clear and cogent description of ancient Hebrew divination practices in the first half of the book. It also includes many beautiful gems that can be sprinkled into any kind of Jewish, Hebrew, or Mediterranean magic, as well as serving as inspiration for almost limitless variations that could enrich virtually any magical or divinatory practice. The second half discusses the Hebrew letters in glorious detail. These are not just "little white book" divination descriptions, but genuine introductions to the spirits of the letters, rich with ideas for nondivinatory mystical and magical use. Even if you aren't inclined to use them for divination, just the introduction to the letters and their inherent magic is well worth the price of the book. Elisheva's long practice, deep knowledge, and genuine love for these topics shines through on every page. I feel lucky to have encountered her work when I was first starting to forge my own Jewish/Pagan practice twenty years ago, but I wish I'd had this book then, too."

—Sara Mastros, author of *The Big Book of Magical Incense*
and *Orphic Hymns Grimoire*

"Elisheva Nesher lays out a fascinating Neopagan approach to lot-casting using the letters of the Hebrew alphabet, taking inspiration from the images that the Hebrew letters or their names initially represented—like Bet for house or Aleph for bull. I especially liked the encouragement to spend twenty-two days meditating on the meaning of each letter, as well as all the knowledge that she shares with respect to each letter's meaning, which would be helpful in any practice that involves using the Hebrew alphabet."

—Harold Roth, author of *The Magic of the Sword of Moses*

"As a witch, I am always interested in new approaches illuminating ancient traditions. Elisheva Nesher's *Casting Lots* is a very sophisticated book and contains many gifts for diviners working in any divination system. While the book is entirely respectful of Hebrew tradition, the work of casting lots is also open to people who are not of Hebrew heritage. The Hebrew alphabet is a foundational part of Western culture, thanks to later traditions based on the spiritualities of the ancient Near East.

Elisheva's chapters on ethical divination and working magic in partnership with the Hebrew letters and their associated divinities are so brilliant that they should be required reading for all diviners, especially professionals. Best of all, the book's wisdom about the ancient Hebrew letters, the tribes, and their traditions are expressed simply and clearly. *Casting Lots* is a must-read for diviners of all types, and for anyone interested in the pre-monotheistic spirituality of the ancient Hebrews."

—Caroline Kenner, cofounder of
The Fool's Dog Tarot app company

CASTING LOTS

Ancient Hebrew Divination Magic

ELISHEVA NESHER

foreword by

DIANA L. PAXSON

WEISER
BOOKS

This edition first published in 2022 by Weiser Books, an imprint of
Red Wheel/Weiser, LLC
With offices at:
65 Parker Street, Suite 7
Newburyport, MA 01950
www.redwheelweiser.com

ISBN: 978-1-57863-709-6
Library of Congress Cataloging-in-Publication Data available upon request.

Cover and text by Sky Peck Design
Cover photograph © Elisheva Nesher
Typeset in Warnock Pro

Printed in the United States of America
IBI

10 9 8 7 6 5 4 3 2 1

We all stand on the shoulders of our ancestors, so I owe gratitude and thanks to the teachers of our spiritual tradition whose values and thinking helped shape mine. This book is dedicated as well to the man in my heart, who has always supported and encouraged me to write. I also dedicate it with thanks to the many people who have, or are still helping me in this project and/or lending their moral support and encouragements: Diana, Judika, and the lot casting groups who have patiently sat through my lectures for years and helped me frame much of what I had to teach in a way more accessible to people outside Israel.

Contents

Foreword

"This is Elisheva Nesher. Her Heathen friends told her you would be here, and said she has to meet you—"

I looked up, blinking, from my first cup of coffee. Still jet lagged from the shift from California to Ohio time, I had groped my way from my cabin to the building where the Winter Star festival was providing caffeine. Standing before me I saw my friend Laurel, a statuesque blonde, and beside her a very fit-looking woman with bright dark eyes and a cap of short black hair.

"She asked if I was the Troth elder who will be speaking at the festival, so I brought her to you," Laurel said. "She's from Israel, and she casts the Hebrew lots like we cast the runes."

Suddenly I was wide awake. The three of us spent the next few hours talking shop, comparing and demonstrating concepts and techniques for divination. Elisheva Nesher and I have been learning from each other ever since. In that first discussion, we realized that reconstructionist Heathens and Hebrews, both of whom come from warrior cultures in marginal environments, have a lot in common, starting with the fact that Aleph, the first sign in the Hebrew alefbet (alphabet), and Fehu, the first rune in the futhark, both indicate "cattle."

That meeting was the beginning of a friendship of over twenty years, one that has deepened through regular meetings at festivals such as Sirius Rising and Pantheacon, visits to each other's homes, and, more recently, conferences on Zoom. During those years, I have learned to value her as a trusted colleague as well as a dear friend, and one of the wisest women I know. One of the topics we often discuss is how to teach others what we do. My own book, *Taking up the Runes,* was published in 2005. Ever since we met, I have been encouraging Elie to write her own book about casting the lots that bear the Hebrew letters, and here it is at last!

What are the lots, or the runes, really? When do we go to them for counsel, and why? Like the runes, the letters of the Hebrew alefbet have a history of use for magic, as well as for communication. Each sign carries its own weight of meaning, as well as the energy it has acquired over centuries of use by people in need.

Elisheva first encountered the lots when she started her service in the Israeli security forces, where they might be cast when all other wisdom failed. After she moved to the US, she had a career in international business communications and then she trained as a therapist specializing in PTSD. Her varied experiences in war and peace have given her a unique and valuable background from which to judge what the lots are actually trying to say.

Over the years, when my own problems have sent me to the runes so often that they are getting tired of answering, I have asked Elisheva for a lot casting. The runes are my constant friends and advisors, but the lots have a powerful energy. As I read Elisheva's book, I can feel them beginning to stir in my awareness, as direct and brusque as the Hebrew language itself, but strong and sure. Those who have a connection to Hebrew culture will feel a family welcome, but those who do not may find in them, as I have found in my friendship with Elisheva, the strong support of an ally.

So, what will you find here?

Interpretation of the symbols in any system of divination is improved by a knowledge of the culture from which it came. Elisheva, who grew up working the land in a kibbutz and has travelled widely in both Israel and the surrounding regions, as well as studying archaeology in Tel Aviv at the Department of Ancient Middle Eastern Studies, draws on this background to present the origin and evolution of the Hebrew script, the development and function of lot casting in the Old Hebrew culture, the role of the ancestors and spiritual powers in the original polytheistic religious system in which the lots were cast, and the shophtim and seers who used them.

With this as a foundation, the book moves to spiritual and psychological preparation, from creating an appropriate sacred space to making a connection with the Otherworld, and finishing with a discussion of ethics, topics based on Elisheva's many years of experience teaching lot casting to students, as well her standing-room-only presentations of lot casting in a ritual setting at festivals.

Thus prepared, the student is ready for the sections that present the lots themselves. Like the runes, each Hebrew letter has a sound, a shape, and a meaning. Their names are drawn from the earliest strata of Hebrew tradition. Just as interpreting a rune draw requires you to learn what the name of each rune means in the context of Old Norse culture before you explore what it means today, to understand the lots you need to know something about the land and culture from which the Hebrew letters came.

Elisheva's discussions of the lots opens a new world. Even if you don't use them for divination, meditating on their meaning can lead to new and fascinating insights from a culture that made a significant contribution to our own. Some of the lot names, like Gimel, the camel, are obvious in a system based on the culture of the Near East; but others, like Quf, the monkey mind, offer unexpected opportunities for insight. The verses that begin each section encapsulate the meaning. The meditations enable the reader to internalize the information.

For the lots to speak fully, they must be used. From her years of experience as a reader and shophet, Elisheva draws examples of how the lots have been interpreted in actual readings and how they can be used in rituals for transformation and healing. The story of how the lot Bet became the focus of a ritual for a woman who had been adopted is especially illuminating. The sample readings demonstrate how the lots can work together to tell a story.

So let Elisheva welcome you to the world of the Hebrew lots, and may Gimel carry you safely from the confusions of Quf to Lamed.

—Diana L. Paxson

Introduction

For the longest time, people have asked me to write a book about lot casting, to share this ancient Hebrew method of divination, meditation, and magic. And for a long time, I resisted. I was unsure if I was the right person for the task. Unlike mentoring, which I have done regularly over the years, or teaching verbally and in person, writing about the Hebrew lots and their many uses seemed daunting: It meant trying to step into the large footprint of people whose examples and teachings over a span of thousands of years have been the soil in which lot casting is rooted.

I use the term "teachers" very broadly. By it, I include many ancient literary sources—such as the Hebrew Bible, Hebrew commentaries, and Hebrew and Jewish folklore. Teachers are also people, both ancient and modern—the romanticized heroes of the Bronze Age whose tales many Israelis grew up with from childhood—for example, Samson, Deborah the prophetess and war leader, and Ehud the chieftain from the biblical Book of Judges. I consider some very real people of recent times to be teachers, too—beginning with the Jewish pioneers who, around the 1800s, fed up with their minority status in Europe (which was at best belittlement and at worst outright persecution), at last said nay to their continued suffering and humiliations, turned their backs to the countries where the mistreatment took place, and returned to the land of Israel.

My use of "teachers" includes also their modern descendants whom I myself have met; all people who, like their biblical ancestors, sweated and tilled the land and dug canals and guarded their fields and flocks of sheep and, above all, who healed the long-neglected land by planting what eventually became millions of trees. This made it easier for them to relate to ancient tribal ancestors who also were shepherds and warriors and farmers, rather than to the estimable and erudite rabbinical scholars bent over ancient parchments in dark rooms.

"We will heal the land," they sang, "and thus by Her we will be healed." Another song they taught us as youngsters sums up these sensibilities:

שירו שירו שירו לארץ
שירו שירו שירו לאדמה
שירו שירו לעלאם כולו
שירו שירו שירו לחיים

Sing sing sing to the Land
Sing sing sing to the Earth
Sing sing to the whole world
Sing sing sing to all Life.

And finally, by teachers I also mean the valuable information offered by the more recent insights of modern scholarship deriving from archeology and modern studies of the Hebrew Bible, which gave rise to the documentary hypothesis. Briefly stated, this recognizes multiple authorships of the Bible, as well as heavy redaction of the biblical text over time, and which also recognizes the evolution of the concept of the Hebrew and Jewish god from polytheistic to monotheistic.

A caution to the reader: There are thousands of books on these topics and I, myself, have read hundreds of them. You will find some of them in this book's recommended reading section. This recent, secular information regarding the ancient Hebrews and the Hebrew Bible was previously unknown and at times it contradicts many now-deeply rooted Western assumptions about ancient Israel, its history, and religion. Such assumptions have permeated Western culture for centuries, to the point of becoming "reality" even for the secular. When, in the past, contradictions in the Hebrew Bible were noticed, they were—and often still are—discounted, dismissed, or often even deliberately ignored by some traditional Western religious teachers and authorities.

Regarding translations: It does not help that traditional religious interpretations, rather than historical or cultural information, frequently bias translations, which have often been written during times when understanding of the ancient Middle East was virtually nonexistent. This in turn affected people's understanding of what the Hebrew Bible text actually means. Nor does it help that dozens of translations of the Hebrew Bible exist—some even from the original Hebrew!—some quite ancient, which further confuse the picture. Errors of translation are usually hard to spot in, say, an English text, but are often remarkably noticeable in the Hebrew text.

And so, in this book I have made my own translation of Hebrew Bible quotes, since, as an Israeli, I am fluent in modern Hebrew. Many years ago in Europe, I also trained as a translator and interpreter, earning a master's degree. In addition, I will offer some recommended reading and sources as part of this work, both biblical and secular scholarly, since the influence of conventional thinking about topics such as the Hebrew Bible or the development of monotheism is so powerful and pervasive that even the well informed are frequently surprised by the information I will share with you in this book. You may be startled and even sometimes shocked when new information contradicts long-held opinions. But I believe it can be to our advantage to see new horizons.

Lot casting for divination, meditation, and magic is currently practiced in my spiritual path, which is called AMHA. This is an acronym for Am Ha Aretz (עם הערץ in Hebrew), meaning "People of the Land"—a Pagan (i.e, not monotheistic) path considered reconstructionist, in that it involves mythopoetic reconstructions of the ways and culture of the ancient Hebrew tribes before the development of Jewish monotheism. We follow "The ancient customs the way they should have been," to paraphrase my friend, author Diana Paxson.

Although our tradition is modern, the name AMHA is an old term, dating back to the first centuries of our era. Loosely translated, it means "hayseed" or "hicks"—ignorant country folk. This was a derogatory term, used in rabbinical literature of the 2nd century CE to express contempt for the nonliterate people of the countryside, those who knew nothing of book religion but clung to simple folk stories, tribal rituals, and ancient beliefs. This view of their ceremony and rituals is expressed by the common rabbinical aphorism, "Customs of the people, unworthy of sages"

To avoid confusion, I might explain here that if you have been to Israel, you may have heard people use the term AMHA for themselves. They are not necessarily on our spiritual path. What they are saying is that they are neither interested nor well versed in religion, preferring folklore. Some will add that they do not bother their pretty heads with the complexities of Jewish rabbinical religion.

We say much the same.

So this is not a book of religion, even though you will see ample use made of the Hebrew Bible, which, to us, is simply a collection of our folk tales, most of which date to long before literacy—to the Middle Eastern Bronze Age and before. Many of those stories (excepting later additions and redactions) were probably first told around our ancestors' campfires when the Hebrews were still semi nomads, then were handed down for generations—long before a small group of priests, some from the south and others from the north of the country, wrote them on scrolls that were in turn eventually conflated, redacted, collected, and made into a book—the Bible.

Many of us ignored the boring lists of the Bible or all the prohibitions written by angry priests. Instead, we loved the stories of travels and adventure, murder and adultery and war, rituals and magic practiced by warriors and seers, stories about ordinary men and women, as well as about those who were prominent among the tribes. We heard these tales as children, as we, too, sat around the campfires. The past was vivid. So vivid that as children, we played at Hebrews and Romans, and of course the Hebrews always won.

Such handed-down stories of preliterate societies contribute to the formation of group memories, so they shape culture, identity, values, and traditions the way soil shapes the life of a tree. To understand the messages and energy that emerge while using lots, we need to understand the soil in which they grew, so much attention is given in this book to the cultural and historical context of lots and their uses.

A clarification of terminology is needed: We are often asked why we call ourselves Hebrews instead of Jews. This distinction was first drawn by rabbinical scholars in ancient times, and is still used by secular scholars today.

- The word "Hebrew" (עברי Ivri) refers to our ancestors before monotheism or, today, to people who chose adoption into AMHA, the name of our spiritual path.

- Followers of the rabbinical tradition, a monotheist path, are referred to as "Jews" or Yehudim (יהודים).

Those of us in AMHA are earth oriented. Most of us are devotees of the Divine Feminine in its various forms and/or of powers in the ancient Hebrew/Canaanite pantheon, which is discussed in the pages that follow. Lot casting reflects this cultural background. Some of us in AMHA are agnostics, and we value that view, too, because we value practice (orthopraxy), especially communal practice, far more than "correct" belief (orthodoxy). For those who have been told that there is no right living without religion, as well as for the general reader, there is a discussion of ethics for lot users later in this book.

One lesson clearly conveyed by the folk tales we grew up with. and that is useful to remember when using lots, is that none of the heroes of those ancient tales we were so excited about as kids could be in any way called perfect; lots remind us of this, too. We are humans and, as such, are not intended to reach some imaginary concept of perfection. It is good to remember this and to remind those for whom we may cast lots.

By far the most powerful lesson on our path—and our highest AMHA value—is that we are open to all. Joining our path by choosing adoption into one of our tribes—or even practicing some of our rituals without joining (like using lots, for example)—is in no way limited to people of our own ethnic roots. For one, we know today that ethnicity is a social construct and, as such, is learned. Also, like many (if not most) ancient tribes around the world, we readily welcome people—any people—with whom there is affinity, who get to know us and who are willing to respect and share in our culture and customs and values. As the matriarch Ruth said so well about inclusion into a new tribe:

Ruth 1:16 (my translation and abridgment):

Where you go, I will go . . . your people shall be my people . . . your gods my gods . . .

And from Leviticus 19:34 (my translation from Hebrew and abridgement):

For you should love the stranger, for you yourself were a stranger in Egypt.

So welcome to sharing the ancient wisdom of our lots. You do not need to join our path, and you do not even need to know Hebrew to use them. In this book, you will find what you need to learn their use.

1

Using Lots

A set of lots consists of twenty-two Hebrew letters, each inscribed on glass, wood, bone, terra-cotta, or stone. Each letter has layered meanings. It is preferable that they be made of natural materials, but lots should be made in spirit, so an exception is made for polymer clay because of the extensive work required to manufacture them from that material, which itself can be meditative.

You can make your own lots; though it's best to learn about them first so that they can then be made in ritual. Lots have a variety of traditional uses: they are used not only for divination but also for meditation and magic. Reverence and focused will and intent are needed whenever lots are cast and for whatever purpose they are used.

In preliterate days, lots typically had pictures on them, rough quick sketches of the objects they were to represent. With time, the pictures became brief stylized symbols of Hebrew letters. The current names of these letters still retain the meaning of the objects they were originally intended to represent. For example, the letter ב (typically spelled *Bet* in English*) when pronounced

---

* It should be noted here that the English spelling of Hebrew letters, and Hebrew words in general, is far from consistent in the various sources; a fact due primarily to the differences between the respective alphabets.

in Hebrew, sounds very close to the word *beyt,* which in modern Hebrew still means house, home, or sometimes family clan or ancestral lineage.

Because of the link between the names of the Hebrew letters and the items they represented, it has been possible to reconstruct with a degree of accuracy what each lot's ancient meaning must have been. Perhaps it is worth noting that, even so, over the centuries, opinions regarding the meaning of each letter has shifted. AMHA interprets them as closely as possible to the objects each of them denotes.

The mechanics of casting lots is simple: Lots are most often held in a bag or sometimes a box, and then they are cast (gently tossed) onto a casting cloth (natural fibers are preferred). When using them, we first prepare ourselves and the space by purifying and or consecrating it for the Working, be it divination, meditation, or magic.

We focus Will and Intent and reach for the Power(s). (I've capitalized these words to indicate that they have metaphysical meaning.) If casting lots for divination, we ask the question that has been on our mind or on the mind of the person for whom we are casting. We pour the lots out of their bag onto one side of the casting cloth. Without looking, we pick out three of them, which we lay in a line. They are then read from right to left in keeping with Hebrew tradition. The Hebrew language is also read from right to left. Because lots harken back to tribal days, any practice involving lots retains some shamanistic elements. What this primarily means is that the seer's energy and their moving of energy to connect to Otherworld powers is the most important element when using lots.

Therefore, except for the initial purification/consecration/ blessing of ourselves and the space, it is not important in which sequence the next steps are taken: Whether you ask the question first, or focus Will first, or pour out the lots on the cloth first matters little. If the energy moves, that is what matters. When using lots, learn to perform the sequence of steps in the way that feels best to you.

Once again: You don't need to be able to read Hebrew to successfully cast lots. As with other forms of divination, it's only necessary to learn what each lot means and symbolizes and to understand a little about their cultural load. Once you have learned their meaning, lots are easy to use.

NOTE: Lots are considered sacred objects. Please consider this, should you wish to take up their use, and handle them appropriately. Treat lots with respect. Do not hand them to kids or pets to play with, nor should they be used during a party for fun. The use of lots is an act of reverence for the wisdom and energy that the Powers agree to share with us. If we keep this in mind, and learn them well enough to be sufficiently fluent in their use to longer need to refer to the book each time we cast, the fullness of their rich meaning unfolds.

As said, we use lots today not only for divination, but also for meditation and for magic, which are further discussed later in this book. Reverence and focused Will and Intent are also needed for those uses of lots, as well as for any other uses of them.

2

Divination via Lot Casting in Antiquity

The Hebrew tribes were not the only tribal people who practiced lot divination. Long before writing, nomads and semi-nomads, as well as sedentary tribes across the globe, used tools of divination to establish a connection to powers (god-forms or spirits) as they understood them. Their diviners—who sometimes were their tribal spiritual specialists—connected to the metaphysical world to find answers or guidance for their communities. A wide variety of divination devices were and are used, usually made from materials at hand: for example, animal bones such as yak knuckles among the Siberian tribes, camel bones among some Middle Eastern peoples, or shells among coastal tribes around the world. Meanwhile, the Scandinavian and Germanic people drew runes for divination, among other purposes.

Divination also flourished in other so-called "more advanced" ancient civilizations, such as in ancient Mesopotamia. First in Sumer, then in Akkad, and later in Babylon, divinatory priests observed the stars and planets and developed a vast literature of astrological divinations and omens to aid magical healing. This was recorded in cuneiform script on clay tablets (sometimes baked, so as to achieve a measure of permanency, if thought sufficiently important). These tablets have survived to our day, and there are so many of them that archaeologists are still translating them.

The Etruscans in Italy were famous and respected for their extensive divinatory literature, from star observations to observations and interpretations of the livers of sacrificed animals to the flight of birds—all recorded in the Sibylline books (now lost) that were studied by the Romans. The emperor Claudius was said to have translated them from the Etruscan, but his translations have unfortunately vanished, too.

The Greek Temple of Apollo in Delphi was presided over by a seeress known as the Pythoness; nobles and envoys of kings from everywhere in the Mediterranean world traveled all the way there to ask questions and get answers.

The divinatory practices mentioned above are not consigned to the graveyard of history, however. People in traditional societies still use them; in the West, there is a resurgence due to neo-Pagan movements, and we AMHA use them today.

That ancient Hebrews used lots for divination is a matter of written record, primarily the Hebrew Bible. Some examples are offered in chapter 3. As wandering tribes, they too would have used materials that are easy to come by: stones, wood, broken kitchen pottery, for example. It is of course possible that when the Hebrews settled down and the traditional cult was eventually centralized and limited to the temple in Jerusalem, the lots used by the high priests might have been fancier, made perhaps of more valuable materials such as glass or stone (considered to be inherently pure) or semiprecious stones or even bronze, silver, or gold.

The practice of lot casting continued, with variations, from Bronze Age nomadic times (c. 3300–1200 BCE) to well into the

2nd century of the Common Era—at a minimum, a span of at least three thousand years. Our earliest Hebrew documentation is in the Bible stories about the migrating Hebrew tribes. Much later, on the ancient fortification of Masada (c. 66 CE), the Hebrew insurgents used lots made of pottery shards; the latest use of Hebrew lots (before they were revived in modern days, sometime around the mid-1800s) is recorded by the historian Josephus Flavius, a Jewish nobleman and military commander, born in 37 CE, who turned his coat and joined the Romans.

The Claim of Unbroken Tradition

Many groups of alternative spirituality claim that their practices and beliefs go back millennia, even as far as Neolithic times, continuing in an unbroken line. The practice of lot use has solid, ancient roots, but I make no such unbroken-line claim.

We can truthfully connect lot casting for divination to the ancient Hebrew tribes, as this is documented in the Hebrew Bible, but over the millennia, rituals and magic evolve. Today, in using lots, we blend what we know from ancient literature with what modern scholarship, including archeology, can tell us about the culture, rituals, and customs of our ancient ancestors. This aids us in better understanding lot messages, since they are rooted in the culture from which they grew.

As I mentioned in the introduction, it may come as a surprise to many that the ancient Hebrews (עברים) did not start out as monotheists. Modern scholars will tell you that the ancient Hebrew belief system was very close to those of the Canaanites. The Hebrews and Canaanites were so closely related culturally, in fact, that the Hebrew language is seen today as a Canaanite dialect.

Because the ancient Hebrew semi-nomads were illiterate, and because, according to scholars, in Israel even by the 6th century BCE, barely 2 to 3 percent of people could both read and write, lots at that time could not have consisted of the entire Hebrew alphabet that we use today.

To start with, to tell the lots apart and read their meanings, each individual lot must have had a different shape or color; perhaps a little later, each began to have some distinctive marks on them; later still, came sketches to signify objects of everyday use, thus serving the purpose of a people who mostly could not read.

We know that Hebrew writing developed from the stylized pictures that eventually morphed into the Hebrew alphabet. An example is "Aleph," which originally was the design of a bull's head; it then became stylized and rotated ninety degrees (all Hebrew letters did over time and nobody really knows why). Eventually, the scratched outline of a bull's head became the letter Aleph* that we see today.

The Hebrew alphabet consists of twenty-two letters. We use all of these when lot casting. Five of the twenty-two letters, though—Mem, Nun, Tsadiq, Pe, and Kaf—have a different form when they occur at the end of a word. For ease of use, we omit these final forms. Lots we use today employ modern Hebrew script (known as "square script" because most letters fit into a square), rather than the ancient archaic fonts that few people can now read.

---

* This may be spelled in English as either Alef or Aleph. It is a problem of transliteration that frequently occurs when transcribing Semitic alphabets into English.

3

Divination and Lot Casting in Ancient Hebrew Literature

L ot casting was not the only Hebrew form of divination for which we have written (by which I mean mostly biblical) record. The oldest literary sources (e.g., the Hebrew Bible) tell us that no less a figure than Abraham found counsel in divination. In *Bereshit* (בראשית, i.e., Genesis) 13:18, it says (my translation and abbreviations):

Then Abram* moved his tent . . .
and went to live near the great trees of Mamre at Hebron.
There he built an altar to the Lord.

To better understand this heavily redacted text, we need to know that in arid areas like Hebron, goats eat all shrubs and saplings so thoroughly that tall trees are rare. So locations with great trees, and especially groves, have been enclosed and protected and the trees tended, which almost certainly indicates sacred use. And, indeed, groves are well known to be locations of worship. To this day, Bedouins in the Sinai approach some clusters of trees with much trepidation at night, fearing the spirits that still reside there.

---

* For those unfamiliar with the biblical narrative, two forms of the patriarch's name are used: Abram and Abraham.

The grove of the oak trees of Mamre was such a location. Building an altar as Abram (Abraham) did, as described in the verse above, most likely consisted of erecting a stela: that is selecting a rock and standing it upright to symbolize a god or simply the presence of the sacred. This act of reverence is also performed by several other patriarchs, as attested to several times in the Hebrew Bible; for example, when Yaacov (Jacob) has a fight with a numinous being in Genesis 32:22, he erects a stela to mark the area as a sacred location; while in Genesis 35:20, he erects a stela over Rachel's tomb. Such stones were raised to mark a site sacred, even if in a remote desert location; or, back to Abraham (Genesis 13:18), to express respect for the power residing in the grove of Mamre, where later, divine visitors tell him, his wife Sara will conceive.

The text describes the message that the god who resided in that grove gave to Abraham. It does not tell us which god was revered there. As I said previously, the ancient Hebrews were not monotheists. Later, when the shift toward monotheism began, redactors probably assumed that the god El (the name of the highest Hebrew/Canaanite god) was the one there. Alternatively, it could have been Yah (which, by tradition, we write instead of Yahweh, a god initially described as one of the sons of El and later conflated with him, as the Bible text show especially clearly when read in Hebrew). Or it could have been any of the senior or junior gods/goddesses revered by the Hebrews and Cananites.

By what method Abraham induced the resident god to talk to him is not spelled out. Nor do we know if the god spoke to Abraham directly or through the mediation of a seer. Very possibly, lot casting, being an ancient practice and widely used, was on that occasion performed by a resident priest or priestess, interrogating the divine on Abraham's behalf. Or perhaps lots were cast by Abraham himself and the god/goddess of the sacred grove spoke to him directly. Abraham was an elder, and in tribal societies, it is often elders who do the divining. That detail, if ever recorded, would have been censored by later redactors.

The Hebrew tribes continued to practice divination: they would later cast lots while roaming the desert in an effort to return home to the land of their ancestor Joseph after having fled servitude in Egypt. An example of this is found in the book *V'yikra* (ויקרא/Leviticus) 16:5,7–10, with a description of ritual lot casting happening well before the Hebrews crossed into Israel. It was part of an important ceremony, a central component of the ritual of the scapegoat: casting lots to determine which of two goats was going to be sacrificed to the god and which was to be chased into the wilderness carrying away the sins of the tribe. From the complexity of the ritual, one can tell this magic practice was not new.

V'yikra 16:7–10 (translation and abridgement are mine):

> *Aaron shall take two male goats and let them stand before*
> *the god* [here, too, this is probably El, the main but not
> the only god] *at the entrance of the Tent of Meeting.*

> *And he shall place lots upon the two goats, one lot marked*
> *for the god and the other marked for Azazel.**

> *Aaron shall bring forward the goat designated by lot for*
> *the god, which he must offer as an offering of atonement*
> *for sins;*

---

* Azazel is the wilderness of the desert to which the designated goat would be driven to carry off offenses to the gods by the tribes.

While the goat designated by lot for Azazel shall be left standing alive before the god, to (later) be chased off into the wilderness.

It is clear from this text that the choice of which goat went where was established by lots, whose answers were determined by numinous power, thus confirming lot casting as a theurgy—an event in which godforms are involved in human affairs.

Moreover, one can tell from the story that the ritual was so well established that describing it, as I did earlier, as three thousand years old may be a conservative estimate.

4

A Brief History of Lots

In earliest times, lots were used in a variety of ways. One long-lived method involved the use of two lots only, for questions requiring only yes/no answers. As there was not yet written language, stones or terra-cotta shards of different colors or shapes or materials or with different marks on them—one to indicate "yes," the other "no"—may have been used.

Such a system was probably used in Joshua 7:14–20 when Joshua and the tribes were searching for a man who had violated tribal customs by keeping treasure he had looted after battle, rather than gifting it to a god.

Joshua 7:14-20 (my translation and abridgments):

Tomorrow morning, all people are to gather near the Holy Tent. Then come forward, tribe after tribe, and the god* will show which tribe is guilty. Next, each kinship group within that tribe must come forward, and the god will show which one is guilty. Next, the families in that kinship group must come, and the god will point out the guilty family. Finally, the men in that family must come, and the god will point out which man did this.

---

*   Again, a reminder that, as the most senior god, El would likely have been the god referred to; but it could also refer to Yahweh or other children of El, or another god/goddess entirely.

Clearly here, the question asked of the lots was not "Who did this?" but rather phrased in such a way as to lend itself to a yes/no answer: "Did this tribe, group, et cetera do it?" Each lot casting further narrowed down the options—all the way to the individual who was the culprit.

Something similar may be the method described in the Book of Samuel. By then the tribes have returned and settled in their homeland and the need for a king was felt. The seer Samuel is charged with identifying the man most suited to become king. Here again, one can see that lots were used to "ask of the god"

1 Samuel 16:1, 5–6, 8, 10–11, 13 (my translation and abridgments):

The god said to Samuel (the Prophet), "I am sending you to Jesse of Betlehem. I have chosen one of his sons as king."

*Samuel purified Jesse and his sons (with a ritual)
and invited them to the sacrifice.*

When they had gathered, Samuel saw Eliay [one of Jesse's sons] *and thought, "Surely the Lord's anointed stands here," but the god told Samuel not to choose him.*

Then Jesse called Ayinaday to walk in front of Samuel. But Samuel said, "The god has not chosen him either."

Jesse had all seven of his sons walk before Samuel, but each time Samuel said, "The god has not chosen these."

*So at last Samuel asked Jesse,
"Are these really all the sons you have?"*

"There is still the youngest," Jesse answered,
"who is tending the sheep."

Samuel said, "Send for him."

Then the god said, "Rise and anoint him; this is the one."

So Samuel took the horn of oil and anointed him [David].

While it is not clearly stated *how* Samuel determined that the god had not chosen the brothers presented to him, the prose and rhythm and the parallel to the example quoted earlier strongly suggest a yes/no technique; again we see the assumption that a god—perhaps their highest one—was the one who determined how the lots would fall.

Among the Hebrews, the practice of lot casting continued as they evolved from nomads to semi-nomadic shepherds following the rains to living in villages or towns. It was presumably used by seers in the smaller temples that, as archeologists tell us, dotted the country, long before the cult was consolidated to Jerusalem around the 6th century BCE. Even then, items called the Urim and Tumim were still in use for divination by high priests in the Jerusalem Temple, who wore them in a pocket or pouch sewn to the priestly garment, indicating their ritual importance. We do not know precisely what those objects were, but since they were used for divination, they probably were some type of lots.

But, clearly, yes/no lot casting is potentially a very time-consuming technique. Of necessity, less time-consuming procedures were eventually adopted. The yes/no method discussed above, while venerable and ancient, is not often used today. Not only is it clunky, but also statistics tells us that one has a 50 percent chance of randomly getting yes or no.

However, there is one type of situation in which it can still be most useful. Say you are not sure how to decide a dilemma: Should you ask for that raise or not? Should you leave a relationship or not?

Take out your yes/no lots. Ask the question and, without looking, pick one of the lots. Then examine your reaction to the answer received. You may have a strong reaction: relief, happiness, disappointment, dislike. Your instinctive reaction may reveal your true feelings, which will allow you to better decide which decision to make.

If you follow this method, please remember that it would be appropriate, at least in our AMHA tradition, to first tell the powers that you are actually asking the question to test your reaction to the answer and thus learn which you prefer. We would not want them to think that you are trifling with them by going off to do the exact opposite of the answer offered. This is simply a courtesy to the spirit forms.

As time evolved, eventually lots bearing personal marks developed, as opposed to the ancient and original two stone method. Each person would have first been told to put their own personal sign on a lot. The lots would then be put in a container, and when the question about who had stolen a goat, for example, got asked, a lot would be fished out of the container with the mark of the culprit on it. This lot-casting method is recorded as having also been used to select an individual for a designated task.

The historian Flavius Josephus wrote in the 1st century CE that the Hebrew rebels on Masada had decided to commit mass suicide rather than be enslaved by the Romans. By that time they could write, at least a little, so they wrote their names on lots to determine which of the warriors was to be the last to survive the mass suicide; he would ensure that everyone was dead before killing himself. Dr. Yigael Yadin, the Israeli archeologist who excavated Masada, wrote in his book that he actually found the lot marked with the name of the Masada rebels' leader.

Divination in Ancient Israel

Contrary to later redactions, in ancient Israel, divination was an accepted practice, and lots were not the only method used. Like many people across the globe, the Hebrews used other methods for divination as well, such as necromancy; that is, contacting the souls of the departed. Given the fact that there was not, either then or now, a belief among the Hebrews or their descendants that the spirits of the dead can be evil or dangerous to contact, spirits of ancestors or spirits of departed wise people would be the ones asked for answers. This was the method used by the wisewoman of En-Dor (mistranslated as "witch of Endor" in the King James version of the Bible). The Hebrew word used is not "witch" but something like "wisewoman," a person operating as a medium or seeress. She was asked by King Saul to interrogate the soul of the dead prophet Samuel for advice.

We do not know if she cast lots or used scrying in a bowl of water or poured oil on water to read the patterns. Both water and oil-reading practices are still used in the Middle East today, usually by older female family members. The Bible text has the king reassuring her because supposedly consulting the dead was evil witchery, forbidden by law, but this appears to be a later, monotheist interpolation. What we do know is that the wisewoman called up the spirit of Samuel the prophet to give guidance to King Saul, who had been scared out of his mind by seeing the size and armament of a Philistine warrior encampment.

1 Samuel, 28:5–7, 11, 13–14 (my translation and abridgments):

When Saul saw the (size of the) camp of the Philistines, he was very afraid.

So Saul asked of the Lord* ... *but the god did not answer him—not by dreams* [one of the ways in which the god(s) made contact with humans] *nor by Urim* [the divination method used by the priests—as said above, probably lots] *nor by other seers.*

So Saul instructed his servants, "Find me a woman who is a seeress, so that I may go to her and inquire of her." (His servants answered, "There is a woman who is a seeress and she lives in En-Dor.")

The woman replied, "Who should I bring up for you?" He (King Saul) said, "Bring up for me Samuel."

King Saul then said to her, "Don't be afraid! But what have you seen?" The woman replied, "I have seen a divine being coming up from the ground!" [Divine in this context does not mean that Samuel was a god but a spirit, hence part of the numinous dimensions.]

Saul said to her, "What about his appearance?" She said, "An old man is coming up! He is wrapped in a robe!" Then King Saul realized it was Samuel the prophet, and he bent his face toward the ground and got on his knees [thus showing reverence for the prophet who was his mentor].

---

*   This phrase, which often recurs in the Hebrew literature, means seeking answers from a godform, not necessarily the main god; i.e., using divination.

All this shows that seeresses as well as seers were obviously in high regard. Later still, in King David's days, the king's faithful champion and general, Joab (Yoav in Hebrew), sent for a wise-woman from the village of Tekoa to help with important political decisions regarding the king's firstborn son Abshalom (2 Samuel 14), which illustrates the important role that all diviners, including lot casters, played in ancient Israel.

Nor was divination reserved only for the use of kings. In 1 Samuel 9, the future king of Israel, Saul, while still a simple tribesman, rides out with a family servant to look for three lost donkeys belonging to his family. After searching for several days, Saul's servant suggests that they consult a lot caster who lives in the countryside nearby who, the servant says, will charge one-quarter shekel of silver to help find the lost animal.

The use of lots retains elements comparable to the shamanistic: that is, practitioners put themselves into an altered state of consciousness and "travel" to the space "in between"—a numinous space that some call the Otherworld. There, they can connect to the energy of "powers" who agree to answer questions by manipulating how the lots fall when cast.

Powers can also be involved when we seek support for other lot Workings, such as meditation or magic. In each case, consecrating the space and focusing will and intention are paramount.

A major difference between modern and ancient lot casting is this: Nowadays, we do not use lots to predict future events. Today, we think that the moment we are told about future events, something shifts the energy and the events will change. Unlike our ancestors in the past, we believe that lots can offer insight or show us where current patterns may lead, but they should not be used to predict specific events.

The Canaanite/Hebrew Pantheon

Contrary to a long-held misconception, fostered by religious establishments for hundreds of years and frequently held even by secular people, the ancient Hebrews did *not* start out as strict monotheists in the sense of modern Christians, Muslims, and Jews. Some (mostly) academic book titles will be offered below as sample literature if you wish more detail.

In addition to what one would call today the senior god-forms or powers, the ancient Hebrews knew of many powers who had many forms and names. Modern secular scholarship, the Hebrew Bible, and also later rabbinical literature attest to this. These powers or godforms were—and are—known collectively as the *elohim*. This is not a name like John or Jack but a masculine plural noun, meaning gods. The juniors among them are also known in the Hebrew Bible as the *"bnei elohim"* (the children of senior gods like El or Ashera), which implies that, being younger, they stood lower in rank than the divine El or his wife Ashera, the ruling couple of the early Hebrew/Canaanite pantheon.

The name *bnei elohim* includes a variety of powers. Because the term was indicative of a multiplicity of gods, referred to sometimes as the council of El, it may well have been baffling for later monotheists or was deliberately obscured; so bnei elohim has been translated in many ways, including in some English translations as "angels" (such as the archangels), who were El's messengers, enforcers, and fighters. But the bnei elohim were junior numinous beings early on, even personified planets and stars, such as the morning star, a "junior" who carries a torch that lights the way for El's chariot at sunrise. Today, AMHA uses the terms elohim or bnei elohim to also include nature spirits, such as the spirits that are trees or that live in trees (the Hebrew word *Ilan,* plural *Ilanim,* means tree, but its grammatical root is the syllable "el," which means divine or god) and any spirits of the land, such as those in or of rocks or rivers; and, of course, ancestors, whom we call Rephaim (רפאים), who have metaphysical protective and healing powers.

We hold the belief today that ancestors sometimes, if they have been gone long enough that people do not recall their faces or names, can choose to revert to nature and become nature spirits or animal spirits, and we can use lots to contact them, if needed. Most often, however, it is they who take the initiative and contact us during a lot casting or meditation. It is probable that the bnei elohim were the powers that people most often asked for answers; in many ancient cultures, asking for answers from the senior powers, especially for common folk, would have been daunting and been reserved for very special, very solemn occasions.

Besides the various bnei elohim mentioned above, the pantheon of the senior Hebrew/Canaanite gods includes:

- אל **El, the father god.** This is the supreme deity. He was also known as "Bull El" among neighboring western Semitic–speaking peoples because the bull was a symbol of power, so a number of chief deities of the region had that attribute. He also represented abundance; having a bull in a herd obviously will increase the number of cattle in the herd (therefore riches as well as power).

    Known also in the past and to AMHA today as the Good God, the Ancient of Days (meaning "Old One," a title of respect), and the God Full of Mercy, Father El is clearly not a smiting god but one that could not be angered, as he is so understanding and good natured. He was the personification of what was then the ideal patriarch. Thus, in the manner of idealized patriarchs, he was most benevolent, slow to anger, and rather a Deus otiosus; that is, a god that is somewhat absent from human affairs.

The name "Elohim" used as a proper name in the Hebrew Bible has a complicated history. The senior god's original title was El Elohim; that is, El god of gods. This was later shortened by the "Yahweh alone" redactors to "Elohim," probably a clumsy attempt to downplay or outright disguise the earlier polytheism.

- אשרה **Ashera or Asherat, El's wife and co ruler.** Like several western Semitic primary goddesses, she is referred to as the mother of all the gods—very likely not intended literally but as an honorific title. Her name, in various spellings, means Mother Goddess in many parts of the ancient western Middle East. Her titles over time included Mother of All the Gods, Star of the Sea, and She Who Walks upon the Waters. Some of her titles were inherited by Mother Mary, a phenomenon common in history.

  The grammatical root of Ashera's name means "abundance, happiness, riches, fertility" (of domestic animals, wild animals, plants, and people).

  Ashera is often depicted holding out her breasts to nourish humanity. (Something that probably titillated the Victorians no end, since, as a scholar friend of mine once told me, they thought it an erotic pose rather than an all-nurturing one.)

Lions, doves, and trees are especially sacred to her. She is, in fact, very strongly associated with trees, especially trees bearing fruits that have many seeds (signifying abundance), such as fig trees, pomegranates, and date palms. The Jewish festival of Tu Be Shevat, when trees in Israel and now elsewhere were and are still planted every year, may have been one of Ashera's holidays. Her most powerful tree symbol, though, is the tree known in Latin as Pistacia palaestina, a subspecies of the terebinth oak, which is a massive, imposing tree, known also as the Elah tree (elah means "goddess" in Hebrew). The modern multi-branched menorah, recorded as being used in the Jerusalem temple and portrayed on Rome's Arch of Titus, which was sculpted to commemorate the destruction and looting of that temple, is a stylized representation of Ashera in the form of her sacred tree.

- עֲנָת **Anat, the warrior maiden** (not virgin, just unmarried). She is a youthful war goddess sometimes referred to in the Ugaritic texts as Baal's lover or twin. She represents some primal instincts, such as battle madness, the chaos and disorder of war, as well as primeval, raw sexual urges. In the Canaanite myths, Anat got her brother Baal out of trouble a few times, wading into battle on his behalf. For Baal's sake, she even threatened the great El once when she was angry. (He, being the good god, did not get angry back. As I said, no smiting for El.)

- בעל **Baal, the young storm and war god.** To dispel a very common misconception, Baal is not a proper name, like John or Jane. It is, instead, a title and means lord or master. Which god was referred to by this title varied by time period and location; different specifiers were used for gods with this title depending on which aspect of him was addressed, which also changed in each local culture. So in the western Semitic world, there were a variety of Baals with a number of names: Baal of the Storm, Baal of the North, or Baal of the Hosts (the holy armies), a title used also for Yahweh in the Hebrew Bible and in Jewish prayers to this day. He was also known as the Thunderer, the Rider of the Clouds, and the Leader of the Heavenly Host (army), who strides in front of the tribes when they go to war. He, not El, is the original smiting god—young, strong, feisty, and often brash and impulsive.

- רחמי **Rahmay, the Womb of All.** Her name comes from a Hebrew root word that means both "womb" and "mercy." Whereas Ashera is the mother of the gods, Rahmay is the mother of all life in nature; though, as often happens in antiquity, the godform attributes overlap, depending on time period and geography. She is the mother of earth personified.

    Rahmay is the sister of Ashera in the Canaanite cycle, also known as the Baal cycle, a series of religious tales that were found in the 1920s in Ugarit, western Syria. Scholars* say that at the time of their writing, Rahmay was already a godform so ancient that she was still both Mother Earth and Goddess of Earth, aspects that later separated.

---

* Othmar Keel and Christoph Uehlinger, *Gods, Goddesses, and Images of God in Ancient Israel* (Minneapolis: Augsburg Fortress, 1998).

- יָהּ **Yah.** There is reason to believe that originally "Baal" and "Yah" were actually the same godform with different appellations among different kinship groups in different geographical locations. Indeed, Yahweh has some of these very same attributes and several of the same titles. (Yah of the North, for example. Lord of the Hosts, which are the heavenly armies—which makes sense for a war god.) Eventually, Yahweh was conflated with old Father El (which can be very confusing when people first hear of this).

As mentioned, AMHA is not a religion but a type of earth-oriented spirituality. Not all AMHA today are necessarily devotees of one or another godform; though all of us, even the agnostics, are devotees of Mother Earth (Em Adama/אָם אֲדָמָה) or of Rahmay, mentioned earlier. Even so, it is nevertheless a custom of our tradition that prior to doing ceremony, formal respects are paid to the powers El, Ashera, Yah, and Anat.

5

Who Were the Lot Casters?

The Gifts of Seers

A certain measure of healthy realism is included in lot practice. It has long been assumed, for example, that the quality and accuracy of the metaphysical message found when using lots is affected greatly by the lot caster's character, relationship to power(s), as well as by their technical proficiency.

In addition to ethics, an old tradition holds that besides successful divination, to be called a seer one has to have received the following gifts. A seer must have the ability to

- hear the message,

- understand the message,

- interpret the message, and

- convey the message to the person asking the question in such a manner that *they* can hear it.

Accuracy is further enhanced by the seer's clarity of soul and mind and, of course, by the seer's experience with this magical tool.

We discourage using lots for divination before learning what they mean, except for the purpose of practicing. Most commonly, during practice, there is some role play; that is, the lot caster in training asks questions for a fellow trainee who plays the role of querent. During training, checking with the book to remind oneself of the lot's meaning is, of course, a necessity. However, the aim for those who wish to become lot casters is to know the meaning of the lots well enough to not need to refer to the book—essentially, to become fluent in their practice.

Experienced lot casters often cast for one or two family members or friends, and they can also cast lots for themselves. But it is wise not to do it for yourself when there are weighty issues. Heavy questions are best answered by others.

Another point to think about when embarking in casting lots for divination is how, as casters of Hebrew lots, we maintain consciousness once contact with the elohim has been established.

Our elohim enjoy being consulted, but some will push to take over more space in the lot caster's consciousness (Anat often tries). Unlike the role of seers in many other traditions, the caster of Hebrew lots is not expected to step aside and lose their here-and-now awareness. The lot caster relationship to the powers is expected to involve a form of mutual respect and consideration, so the lot caster is not a passive tool of the elohim, who do not really much respect that anyway. The lot user must instead be ready to question the lot messages, or even to take issue with the powers—on behalf of themselves, if they are doing a self-casting, or for whomever they are casting. This was Abraham's position, and it is ours.

Even the pushier elohim are believed to most respect a seer willing to push back or at least to stand their ground, and they form the strongest relationship with those who do that. We like to think this is because we consider AMHA a spiritual path of peaceful warriors, but there is a precedent for the "push back," which gave rise to a tradition called "god wrestling."

In Genesis 32:22–32, Jacob wrestled with a being referred to as אִישׁ, which means "man," but elsewhere in the Hebrew Bible, אִישׁ is often also used to mean "warrior," in the sense of a numinous warrior being. Sometimes there is a reference to angels. Translations often use that word, whether it exists in the original Hebrew or not, since over the centuries the awareness that more than one numinous being existed gradually faded into the background. Also, translations have blurred the fact that the different words used for such numinous beings may have originally been intended to mean one or more of the bnei elohim. So Jacob's adversary in the wrestling bout actually refers to one of the powers. Which one is uncertain, but probably a senior god. The wrestling match earned Jacob a broken hip but also earned him a new name (Israel יִשְׂרָאֵל), which, being given by a power, was clearly a reward.

In Hosea 12:4, the same power who wrestled with Yaacov (Jacob) was referred to as מַלְאָךְ, "angel," which confirms it having been one of the bnei elohim.

Another good reason to not let the messages from the bnei elohim totally take us over when casting is that what they say is not always totally clear, and so for a seer to keep at least some of their wits together while doing divination with lots is only good sense.

Who Could Practice?

Historically, the societal role and the degree of influence of people who cast lots, or used any other type of divination or magic, changed over time. Originally, responses from the elohim may have been sought mostly by consulting family or tribal elders of any sex or other people in one's circle acknowledged to have powers of metaphysical connection, so almost anybody, at least occasionally, served as diviners and casters of lots. The use of full-time specialists may have been rarer. Possibly, some of the seers who were working in countryside temples were Levites—that is, people of a priestly caste—but it appears that many were not. There is no evidence of early diviners having to be of priestly lineage, and one most certainly does not have to be today.

While early on, small temples apparently dotted the land, their use gradually faded. The centers of religion moved from country to city as the religion of the Hebrews was centralized and thus controlled from Jerusalem. As to ethnicity, ancient Israel had a highly diverse population, and there is no evidence that the diviners or lot casters all were Hebrews, either. Ancient peoples were usually quite practical, and they would have consulted with whomever was good enough and reliable enough to do the job.

The restriction of the practice to high priests in the Jerusalem temple came much later and was due to a mostly political decision of concentrating the cult in Jerusalem, which elevated the status and role of priests.

Eventually, even the Urim and Tumim of the high priest were forgotten, yet the tradition of the metaphysical potency and/or sacredness of the Hebrew letters is so powerfully old and so embedded in the culture that even the strictly monotheistic rabbinical tradition retains reverence for the letters and their power. The kabbalists from the Middle Ages on chose to attribute mystical power to each of the Hebrew letters, and some today still use them for meditation and kabbalistic magic. But the tribally oriented cultural context was lost, and so was the original nature-oriented celebration of most of our festivals, an earth orientation we have reverted to today. Because our spirit remembers the tribal days, our style of lot casting is rooted in earth spirituality.

What Questions Were Lot Casters Asked?

The topics that people brought to the seers for lot casting were manifold. We mentioned a few notable and dramatic ones earlier. But in antiquity, assistance from lots would have been sought when people wished to know the outcome of harvests, or how to correctly do ritual ceremonies, or what to do to aid human or animal fertility or to avert the anger of powers (as in the case of the scapegoat ceremony). Of course, people also asked if there would be good outcome to an endeavor.

Except for the fact that today, as noted before, we do not predict events, the questions brought to lot casters are not much different. We frequently are asked questions about work, health, career, love, or important choices that need to be made, and people seek advice on all matters of personal importance. It is perhaps a good moment here to emphasize that when advice is offered, the lot-casting tradition does not require one to blindly obey; on the contrary, the powers are consulted to offer their advice, not to issue peremptory orders. We remain free to choose whether or not to follow the advice the lots offer.

The Shophet

Before the consolidation of cult practice in Jerusalem, going outside the tribe or community for a "seeing" was probably not often necessary; as other peoples in the region, one had one's tribal wisemen and wisewomen. But sometimes people sought counsel from a respected seer from outside their own tribe, often traveling great distances. This may have been reserved for special circumstances; for example, if one's local elders or diviners could not provide answers or if questions about issues within the tribe were so politically sensitive that a trusted, presumably impartial, outsider had to be consulted. Their skills would also have been useful if there was discord or a feud between tribes. Some modern Bedouin tribes still use a respected third party as an intermediary to avoid feuds.

In Israel, that prominent person would have been of any sex and was known as a *shophet* (שׁוֹפֵט). This word is translated as "judge" in English, but that word fails to fully capture their function. A shophet would have served not only as a seer but also as a law speaker, battle chief, and mediator who could be called in to judge or resolve intertribal feuds. Sometimes, they would call the tribes to war (see the Book of Judges).

The "job" of shophet was offered by the community to a person who had earned their trust. In some cases, a shophet might have been nominated by another reputable seer who was directed by the gods to do so. It is said that some of the shophtim (plural of shophet) were formally anointed and that after this their eyes "were opened," therefore opening a channel to the elohim in their various forms; but not all shophtim were anointed. Some shophtim "judged over Israel" (held the position of shophet) for many years, which presumably meant that they did their job in a way that pleased the people. It is likely that in those days, as in some tribal groups today, the people who chose them could fire them if dissatisfied.

The stories of the various shophtim in the biblical Book of Judges are often lively and dramatic. One of my favorites was about a prominent female shophet in ancient Israel. Deborah, the prophetess and war leader, seems to have held the position for a long while. Her battle strategies are still studied in today's Israel. It is said that she would sit beneath a (presumably sacred) tree on top of a hill and "judge" the people. The mention of a hilltop and tree points to the location being a "High Place"; that is, a sacred area. A small country temple, or in modern terminology a country chapel, may have also been found on such a location.

The Modern Shophet

This combination of war leader, mediator, seer, and lot caster still exists in our AMHA tradition. The original shophtim from Israel were all war leaders, respected for their integrity and courage. Today, our tradition of lot divination says that the casting should be done for no more than three people. For a group larger than three, lot casting is by tradition performed by a shophet, and very often takes the form of a public ritual. Our tradition's reconstructed ritual is called "Seeing for the Tribes."

As in the ancient past, the modern shophet can be of any sex. The calling to the shophet role does not result from an election in the modern sense. They are named for the job in the ancient way, by group evaluation and group consent.

In literature about shamanistic tradition, it is recorded that the person summoned to serve their community as shaman often felt a call from powers before taking up that role. An example of this is found in Mircea Eliade's book *Shamanism* (Princeton University Press, 1964). A shophet I knew in Israel said they had felt that same call for years; another shared that they had had no such mystical experience. However, just as shamanistic literature recounts, every shophet that I talked to or heard about underwent a traumatic initiatory experience.

6

Lot Divination

Touching the Otherworld

Using lots has some aspects that one could call shamanistic. The act of reaching out to the elohim when using lots for divination or magic or meditation involves a state of trance. Some spiritual traditions hold that you can achieve a trance only if you agree with specific religious beliefs. This is not our position.

There are also traditions that maintain that only specific techniques are the "correct" ones to achieve a meditative state for divination or magic. We disagree with that, too. There are many techniques that have been developed in many cultures over time for attaining a mental state suitable for divination or meditation. Differing ways to focus intent and will for Workings have been handed down from many traditions. It is not within the scope of this book to discuss any of them in detail. There is an overview of our approach later in the book.

Sometimes, people who are starting to engage with a metaphysic practice tell us that they are bewildered by the number of approaches to trance divination or trance meditation. Bluntly stated, we think that they all work if done according to the practices of the particular tradition.

People have also told us that they are afraid of reaching a state of trance; they fear the word itself. It may be that they are influenced by the old dread of being taken over by demons. Or there is an anxiety about opening up. But what is known today is that "trance" is a state of consciousness that all normally functioning human brains are capable of achieving.

Different academic disciplines name it differently. Psychologists, ethnologists, folklorists, et cetera each have their own preferred term for "trance," so these days it comes with a variety of labels: trance, hypnotic state, shamanic state of consciousness, meditative state, sacred state, induced trance state (as in clinical hypnosis) or self-induced state, prayerful state, and so on.

Regardless of label, while their purposes may be different, all these states are pretty much the same neurologically. All involve attaining an altered state of consciousness in which awareness of the here and now is reduced or even eliminated to facilitate reaching the liminal, numinous metaphysical realms. Light trancing is frequently part of lot-casting divination and is, of course, a given when meditating with lots.

When casting for others, experienced practitioners can reach a particular type of trance state we call "shamanistic," because it was first described in the literature about shamanic practices. It involves splitting awareness, frequently described as a "split consciousness," "shamanic state of consciousness," or "dual consciousness."

In this state, part of the lot user's mind goes to the Otherworld(s): the liminal spaces traditionally held to be the ones where the elohim and the seer can meet. The other part of the consciousness remains in the here and now to monitor the proceedings and to talk to the person(s) for whom the Working is being done. When casting for oneself, duality of consciousness is not especially needed—other than perhaps to jot down some notes if one worries about not remembering the answers.

The Role of Powers and Their Answers

In our tradition, the elohim (powers) are believed to always be either neutral or benevolent. They do not lie to us nor mislead us. They do not attempt to harm us. They do, sometimes, refrain from offering clear answers. This is sometimes, in part, because their dimension of existence and ours are sufficiently different that the messages get garbled. Sometimes, the elohim choose to give no answer at all. Occasionally, the energy coming from the lots indicates to the lot caster why this might be happening: Perhaps it is the elohim's way of saying that the asker needs to work a little harder to find the answers, or that the asker already knows the answer and just has to recognize it. Or even that the lot caster (or the person they are casting for) is not supposed to offer answers at this point.

The ancestors are especially helpful. In many cultures around the world, those who are gone from this plane are feared. Measures are taken to prevent them from returning in any way. This is not how our people have traditionally looked at it. Ancestors in ancient times were celebrated, fed, and offered libations at least once a year through the ritual of Marzeach.

Our tradition is that regardless of how nasty Aunt Sally or Uncle Joe may have been in this life, they have left the human "toxic" self behind. Ancestors always have our back. Which is why we often seek answers from ancestors when we cast lots—before attempting to connect to other powers. In our experience, the old ones gladly come to speak to those who respectfully call to them. Among the elohim, they seem the most approachable and the ones most likely to show up in our meditations and most willing to chat and give answers.

People have often asked us: What if I do not know who my ancestors are? For this, we have a simple answer: You may not know who your ancestors were, but they know you.

When doing lot divination, it is important to know that we do not have to aim for a specific power for answers. If will and intent and the appropriate ceremonial respect are present, one or another (or more than one) of the powers will come talk to us. They do like to connect and be connected to.

If we ask for help from specific elohim when lot casting, there is a traditional etiquette involved. To start with, we do not "summon," the powers we seek to contact. They are the powers. We are the humans. They pack a lot more energy. Or, to put it another way, they are, metaphysically speaking, our elders, and in our culture, by custom, the senior is treated with deference. So a junior cannot *demand* that a senior show up and answer questions; it would be considered disrespectful. According to our customs, it always is the junior who visits the senior; that is, we go to the Otherworld liminal spaces where (we hope) the powers are willing to connect with us.

Nor is it our custom to dismiss powers when we feel it is time for the meeting to end. In Middle Eastern culture, you dismiss servants, not those people or powers that deserve your respect. So if we must, we politely take our leave. We certainly don't want the powers to take umbrage. The powers are the ones who end meetings. They will signal that the lot casting is over by letting their own energy fade.

The way this often feels is that the lots have nothing additional to say, and the energetic connection to Otherworld drops perceptibly. Some people describe it as the lots having lost their "charge." When this happens, the experienced lot caster knows that there will be no further answers to the question we asked.

Our next step is to thank them and return to our normal here and now consciousness.

"Respect" for the elohim does not mean groveling, and most of their statements are not commands. Our traditional belief is that powers want us to retain our critical thinking rather than follow blindly what we think they said.

It is best to think of the answers the elohim offer during lot casting as suggestions or insights. It is still up to us to ponder and reflect before moving forward. Another reason to not take everything at face value when asking powers for answers is that powers operate out of space and time as we understand them and without our own human limitations, which is one of the reasons their answers are not always unmistakably clear or their advice feasible in the form in which it is given. We are the ones in charge of understanding what, realistically, is good for us or what may be detrimental. We can ask for clarification, of course. The elohim involved will usually try to clarify.

There are some circumstances in which, as mentioned earlier, it is necessary to actually take issue with them. As mentioned earlier, this is called god wrestling, and Yaakov (Jacob) received his new name by doing just that. He got a broken hip for it, too, which simply means that weighty issues can be painful to tackle. But Yaakov received the name Israel as a gift from the elohim, and the whole event could be seen as an initiation event resembling those of shamanistic traditions.

In any event, when there are doubts caused by what has come to us from Otherworld in a lot-casting answer or meditation, it is a good idea to get a second opinion; that is, consult another reputable seer. It does not matter of what spiritual tradition; choose a diviner of competence and good repute.

Regarding Ceremonial Spaces

When preparing for ceremony, the ritual celebrants or special-ists of some traditions, especially those whose lineages come from Western esoteric practices, usually start with casting a circle. This creates an enclosed, magically protected, dedicated ritual space within which the divinatory or other ritual can then take place.

Originally, in medieval Europe, such circles were intended to contain the entities that were being called up by the magus or alchemist. The Church forbade summoning entities because it was feared that calling up powers could cause one to inadver-tently bring in adverse, or even evil, "demon" forces. In those days, there was a widespread belief in "devils" lying in wait, always ready to pounce. Regardless, the practice continued, so one started by casting circles to be safe. One can think of the circle as a type of magical "cage" to keep the summoned powers safely contained.

The modern circle casting among magic practitioners who reconnect to old European traditions derives from this, but there often is more to it: Casting a circle is not primarily to contain an unwelcome entity who chooses to show up, maybe unbidden, in one's group. Today, the casting of the circle around the individ-ual or the group is to keep negative energies from entering. One can think of it as creating protective walls.

Casting circles is a truly venerable custom and goes way back, far further than the Middle Ages. The earliest examples of the use of circles were recorded in Mesopotamia on cuneiform tablets. The texts speak of creating circles or other geometrical shapes by using salt to enclose the space. The salt lines acted as boundaries, marking where the outer wall of a planned temple complex or its foundations would be, for example. The salt circle or rectangle was intended to purify, sanctify, and/or consecrate while complex incantations were recited. But the point here was to ritually separate the ceremonial space (inside the line of poured salt) from the outside, nonritual one. No averting magic of locking in or locking out evil was intended.

Since Hebrew lot casting is a practice that originated in Hebrew culture, it has no built-in belief of "evil" powers prowling around or lying in ambush to harm people. No concerns were handed down to us of negative energy coming in from outside to disrupt Working(s). We do, of course, acknowledge that a toxic participant may be the bringer of bad energy, but that is a different concern; it's a person, not a power, causing a problem. It could even be ourselves—annoying but certainly not menacing. People can be dealt with appropriately. At any rate, since we have no record of tribal protective circles, we do not cast them today.

Another reason for this—an often-unvoiced assumption—is that a group coming together for a ritual purpose is automatically a "minyan" and that such a group therefore forms an egregore, a ritual force or energy which creates space consecrated to ritual. The same applies to the solo practitioner when lot casting: Will, focus, and intent to connect to the holy ones and, at a minimum, sending them signals of respect when doing the Working is all that is needed.

If the lot casting is a public ritual (the one we call Seeing for the Tribes), the shophet does not cast a circle, either. While the people attending such a public ritual may not feel engaged in a ritual, and hence do not energetically form a minyan (quorum), the lot caster, in this case the shophet, is traditionally deemed to inherently have protective powers of their own. (If they don't have it, they should not be casting lots for the tribes, let alone be shophet.)

By old tradition, people coming to consult with the chieftain/seer in a public lot casting become that shophet's guest and are therefore "under the wing" or "in the shade" of that seer. In tribal days, that protection springing from laws of hospitality was enforced by show of arms, if needed. The intent was to prevent quarrels or even feuds from blowing up while the people were gathered around a shophet for a seeing. Even today, among some Arabian tribes, doing bodily harm to a fellow guest while in the tent of a chieftain is a serious offense to the host, who would then be honor bound to avenge it.

While we do not typically have to worry about feuds causing trouble nowadays, we have had the experience—very rarely, thankfully—of people coming to a public seeing and starting a quarrel—or trying to. It is then the obligation of the shophet to break up the quarrel, preferably, of course, in the most gentle and polite way possible. In all my years of being shophet, I had to evict a person who could not be reasoned with only once. Again, if they can't do that, they should not be shophet.

Ceremonial Spaces for Lot Use

Opinions differ in a variety of spiritual traditions about which space is most suitable for practicing divination or other types of ritual magic.

It is, of course, ideal to have a dedicated ceremonial and/or consecrated space where one can do the Workings. This may be a room that is habitually reserved for that or a space in one corner of a room; it could be a garden or a city park or any other space that one can return to and in which one can focus will and intention and not be disturbed. Ideally, it is a location that is not used by the practitioner for any other purpose.

Such a dedicated space is not always feasible. We have learned over time that it is enough to consistently use a space, even if it as small as a corner of one's room. If one is doing the Workings regularly, it helps raise the energy. Use it for daily meditation, too; whenever possible, it also helps to create a consistent schedule and charges the space. As to what time of the day or night to use lots—anytime it is convenient. We do not require lot casting or lot meditation to be linked to moon or sun phases or planetary movements. Some lot Workings are enhanced by being performed at the full moon or at the dark of the moon, but such choices are not mandatory.

7

How to Handle Lots

Some traditions hold that objects used for divination may never be touched by anyone other than the seer. In this we differ. If you have a newly made set of lots that you are using for the first time, you must be the first one to handle them (apart from whoever made them). Thereafter, as long as their attitude is respectful and they have asked for permission—which you can give or not—anybody you choose can be allowed to hold or touch your lots.

This is because, in our AMHA tradition, lots do not absorb people's energies; lots transfer only the energies from or to powers.

Who Can Use Lots?

This bears repeating: Anybody respectful and willing to learn is welcome, regardless of what other spiritual tradition they may follow.

We do ask polytheists who revere powers from other pantheons to not call on them when using Hebrew lots. You can call on ancestors—we all have them—or on local land spirits or on no specific power at all, if you prefer. But each path has its own high beings and spirit forms; each path also normally has traditional ways in which to interrogate them. It is best not to mix the traditions of one with the powers of another.

We are in no way saying that if you are a polytheist you should stick to one pantheon in your practices. As far as we are concerned, all roads lead to the powers who show us humans different faces; one should feel free to have however many pantheons one can handle (or none). But since each will have traditional methods of divination and magic proper to their cultures, we think that it is polite—and more effective—to address a power in its own traditional divination language. Connect to Thor with runes and to Ashera with lots.

Key Steps in Preparing for Lot Use

As mentioned earlier, there are differing ways to focus ritual intent and will for Workings, handed down from many different spiritual traditions. Here are some of the key elements that we think are helpful for achieving a successful lot trance. Whether doing lot divination meditation or magic, we think it would be useful to consider them. These steps are an overview, and the sequence in which they are done is more common sense and preference than it is a specific order.

- It is a good idea to turn off *all* electronic devices. Do not answer the phone, email, or texts while using lots because it interferes with and disturbs the energy. Lot use means accessing one's sense of reverence for the ritual about to be performed and to the powers, if you have called on any.

- Connect to and gather soul (psychic) energy.

- Hold it together with your ritual will.

- Focus your ritual intention.

- Send that blended energy into the lots before casting or at the start of using them.

- Practice, practice, practice. Success, as in any tradition, will depend on experience.

There are many paths to learning how to enter altered states, and beginners often wonder which one to choose. If you are new to this, there are excellent books that teach a variety of ways on how to achieve a meditative/shamanic/altered state of consciousness. Anyone can find a method and procedure that works for them and find the path on which the journey to an Otherworld destination and connecting to powers become possible.

I recommend Diana Paxson's book *Trance-Portation: Learning to Navigate the Inner World* (Weiser Books, 2008), which is suited to people from any spiritual tradition. There are others on the market, though perhaps not as comprehensive or as deep.

A question often asked of us in AMHA is: Do the methods I have learned from this or that tradition work or which works best? You may be able to guess what our answer is: They can all work. Most human brains function very similarly when it comes to the ability to reach trance states. What differs is culture and tradition, which is why we have ended up with so many different ways and different names for something that is ultimately the same neurological state.

What is needed for lot trance is to use good methodology, to develop an understanding of the culture so as to acquire the "maps" for journeying the AMHA way, and, most importantly, to be consistent in one's practice.

Regardless of method followed, beginners attempting to reach the necessary altered state to do Work must practice. Our neurological systems learn best through repetition. We recommend that a beginner take at least a few minutes daily to work on this.

Working Well with Lots

I have mentioned the important role of culture when doing Workings with lots. This is why so much of our history and tradition is discussed in this book. Ancient custom is the source of the energetic charge carried by the lots and must be heeded. If you can't get in touch with these energies at first, don't worry; that is not unusual for the novice. It takes a while to get "in sync" with your lots and with the beings that speak through them.

The Language of the Lots

The lot language is Hebrew, and although you do not need to know the language to cast lots, you will, however, find that the messages and imagery are more vivid or colorful than what a Westerner may be used to. Remember, the roots of this practice are in the ancient Middle East, where even to this day people's speech is vivid and rich in imagery.

Beside reading an answer, you may also "see" the meaning of your casting as it comes through in pictures, or hear it as words, or you may sense it—or all of the above. Whichever way, what is happening is that you are receiving energy from the lots. How your brain translates it for you, in words or pictures or sensation, really depends on your own cognitive style. That is, it will depend primarily on which of your senses processes energy best. There is no right or wrong about the shape the conveyed message takes. When the lots answer a question with a picture or story, slow down and ponder the details to best understand the meaning; if you hear it, really listen.

Since lot Work is done in a trance state, the more you practice going into that altered state, the faster and easier the connection happens—provided your will and intention are focused and a state of reverence is there.

Here are a few other observations that are useful in preparing for lot-casting divination, many of which also apply to lot meditation and magic.

1. Lot answers can be startling: Lots are blunt in their answers and do not sugarcoat replies. (If you are the seer, you are ethically bound to convey the messages as humanely and respectfully as possible.)

2. Before casting for another, explain that sometimes they will not wish to hear what the lots have to say and to be prepared.

3. When times comes for asking the question, the wording does not have to be totally precise. The asker must simply focus on what they feel they need, no matter the words used; even if they cannot be articulate, the elohim will still know what is on their mind.

4. If there is no specific question or you are not clear about what the question is because of its complexity, you can just ask to be told what it is that you need to hear.

5. The querent should know that they do not have to ask a question aloud. If they are not comfortable sharing what their concern is, tell them to think their question or to mask it a little to protect their privacy.

6.   It is also of value to know that the lots may not answer what the querent asks but instead tell what the Otherworld entities think the querent needs to hear!

This is why sometimes the elohim respond by addressing something entirely different from what was asked. We usually find out at some point, even days later, that there was excellent reason for them to do that.

The Steps for Casting Lots for Divination

It is consistent with primitive magic sensibility that the description of any lot use should not be read as a series of sequential, step-by-step instructions. With practice, one learns what sequence works best. We will share some experiences reported by practitioners; if your is different, it does not mean that you "did it wrong."

Here is a broad outline of how most of us engage in lot use.

We start by taking deep, calming breaths to aid us in reaching a meditative (trance) state. We dab incense oil on ourselves—on wrists, forehead, or back of the hand. We call this "anointing" ourselves, since in our folk tradition, anointing "opened eyes"; that is, gave seers their metaphysical powers. We prefer frankincense oil and/or myrrh oil, because they were in ritual use during ancient times, and their scents consecrated ritual spaces.

If the place is safe from fire hazard, and we prefer not to put perfumes on our skin, we can use incense or other resin that can be burnt on charcoal—or we can use both. But we make sure that we or whoever we are working with does not have a problem with smoke.

Since the repeated use of specific scents creates a type of neurological cue, we encourage selecting one scent for each specific Working, say only frankincense for meditation or only myrrh for lot-casting divination. Some people, however, use the same scent for both.

Some of us use a variety of other scents, dedicating each of them to Workings with a specific power; for example, lilac or attar of roses or a scent of fruit for Ashera. Or, if dealing with ancestors, it could be the jasmine scent that Aunt Sally used to wear or the whiskey she liked to drink poured into a little cup as a libation and later discarded. Some people prefer to not use any scents at all.

Lighting a candle (only if safe!) can also be used to set the ceremonial space. We like those lovely little battery-powered candle lights, especially if we are traveling and doing the Working in a hotel room. Ritual hand washing, with or without scented water, is another option. Do what works for you. You may pick one or several of these methods. However, if at all possible, we use the same procedure, and ideally same sequence, each time we do the same kind of lot Working. This helps create a ceremonial mindset, a ceremonial space, and facilitates a trance state.

The next steps are essential, but they, too, are not listed in a precise order. For example, opening the lot bag can take place before or after the anointing or incense lighting, before or after the person we are casting for has asked their question, et cetera.

At the right moment, we open the lot bag or box.

We take out the casting cloth, unfold it, and lay it down.

We gently pour the lots from their bag onto an upper corner of the cloth. Which side of the cloth we do that on simply depends on whether we are right or left handed.

Some of us like to have on hand the symbols of the powers of which we are a devotee when lot casting, such as an Ashera tree or the picture of an ancestor we like to work with or simply wish to honor. If so, we set them along the top of the casting mat. This step is not a requirement. Sometimes, if the person we are casting for is from a different spiritual tradition, they may be more comfortable if we do not use the symbols of our own powers; since we all have ancestors, they usually are okay with that.

We are now ready to cast. We ask the querent to focus on what they feel they need and then to ask their question.

The Otherworld entities of our tradition are not especially literally minded, so if our querent's question is vague or poorly phrased, it is of no matter as long as we, as the seer, have at least a sense of what the question is about. We can help rephrase if we think it is necessary. Most often, the best questions to ask is simply: "What do I need to know?"

We take deep calming breaths and ask the elohim to meet with us and answer. The energy will tell us when we can proceed.

We gather the lots in the corner of the casting cloth into a small mound without looking at them. If we are using a scent, we usually smell it at this point (and any time we need to boost our energy).

Still without looking, we take three lots from the pile, toss them on the cloth, then order them in a line. Now we can look at them and turn them face up, if needed.

We always read the line of lots the way Hebrew is read; that is, from right to left.

As we do that, we look at each lot and say in our mind what each symbol represents. If we know the little poem for each by heart, we recite it aloud or in our mind. But even just reminding ourselves of what the meanings of each lot is will keep our lot reading grounded, preventing lost focus and/or flights of fancy, which can easily happen in a trance state but can blur answers for even the most experienced lot caster.

While this is going on (or before, or at any suitable stage of this Working), we have been connecting to and gathering our soul energy. We have gathered it and focused ritual will and intention. Most people start their casting by doing this first.

What happens next is described differently by different practitioners. Many of us begin to expand our energy outward, past our skin and farther and farther out, which metaphysically builds the passage to that liminal Otherworld meeting space where powers who help us will manifest. Some lot casters speak of this as building a bridge to the elohim. By continuing to breathe deeply and evenly and maintaining focused intention, we maintain that bridge.

Some of us report that they feel their own gentle but powerful push outward change to a gentle powerful pull, their call from the Otherworld. Many say that this pull is what sustains them on the way to the liminal space. Even beginners who have never felt this before usually know not to be afraid: Reverence protects us as does our just intention, which is ritual; we can remind ourselves that we are doing this either to help ourselves thrive, or we are helping another.

At some point, we are there. We feel the power(s). We know them to be present.

It is not necessary to identify who they are, though some lot casters prefer it. Sometimes we will sense or see or feel their identity—one or more of the elohim, or ancestors, or spirits of the land, or any who would like to offer their support. We have learned that most often the powers who turn up to offer answers or guidance are the asker's own ancestors. But sometimes we only know a power is present. For the ritual of lot use, that it is enough.

When the questions are being answered, the part of our soul that remained in the here and now will begin to speak the lot reading.

We easily know when the powers are done answering; the connection fades as their desire to offer answers is nearing its end.

When we have completed the reading, we ask the person for whom the casting was done if they wish to have anything from the message clarified. If so, we can usually do that without the need to cast again, just from the energy that surrounded the original casting of lots. But if there is a need to cast again, the lots that were used for the first reading do not go back on the pile with all the others; they are set aside somewhere on the table or cloth. We pick three new lots from the pile and cast again.

If no clarification is needed, the lot casting is done. So we say: "This casting is closed." This is a ritual sentence that gently brings down the energy and helps us return fully to the here and now.

At some point during this final step, we thank the powers that have helped with the lot casting and given us answers.

Then we put the lots back in their bag.

The lot casting session is over.

Sometimes, the person we cast for does not like what they heard and wants to keep on asking in the hopes of getting an answer more to their liking. Resist the temptation to do that: The elohim have no objection to a question being asked twice to clarify the earlier answer, but they really dislike being nagged and will rapidly become snippy if you persist.

Ultimately, as the seers, it is up to us to decide whether to cast a second time for the same question. If necessary, we will politely tell the querent no. If we know we are one of those people who cannot say no, we don't cast lots for others.

Sometimes, after closing the casting with the sentence "This casting is closed" but before we have put the lots away in their bag, the person we are doing the Working for asks if they may ask an entirely different question.

In that case, all twenty-two lots go back on the pile. As before, we mix and stack the pile, draw, and cast to get an answer or answers. When done, we thank the powers again, say "This casting is closed," and replace the lots in their bag.

By tradition, we are allowed at most three questions from the same person during one lot casting session; experience has shown us that if we try to ask more, the powers usually decide they have had enough, and the energetic connection fades quite quickly.

It is best not to immediately give a casting to another person. You need to be sure to give yourself some time to rest your mind before resuming. Getting up from the table and taking a few steps away from the chair may be all that is needed. Or going to get a drink of water. Traveling to the Otherworld can be more tiring than you at first realize.

Interloping Powers

As mentioned, by our tradition, we do not call on powers not of our pantheon (ancestors are the exception).

Now, it has happened sometimes that powers we do not recognize show up while we are casting or guiding a meditation. Their energy tells us they are not our traditional elohim, and we may even recognize them as powers known in other pantheons. This happens most often when the person for whom we are doing the Working is a practicing devotee of a power from a different tradition with which they have a strong connection. Occasionally, we will not recognize the power, and their devotee will tell us who it is from our description.

We may be startled when these numinous interlopers show up, but we certainly should do nothing to attempt to stop them. They are powers after all. They sometimes enter after knocking once; though most often, they enter without knocking. Powers do not need our permission. All powers deserve our respect, and if they choose to show up, well they can. We will greet them politely and thank them politely when they go.

We like to believe that when a power from a pantheon other than ours visits our lot Working, whatever diplomatic courtesies they and our own powers feel they owe one another have been properly extended, and they have worked out all the details. Most often, those strange powers who show up have affinity with powers of our own pantheon. Such as, for example, mother goddesses from different traditions. This is another reason why whoever comes will be respected; they come as the guests of our own powers—and besides, they come to assist.

8

The Role of the Lot Caster

In many cultures, seers are thought of as merely channels. While powers transmit their meanings through the seer's vocal cords, the latter's role is seen to be passive and receptive. But cultures differ. In ours, the lot caster has to keep at least part of their mind conscious and fully aware. This is because the powers do not always bother to clearly answer. Sometimes, they even make themselves deliberately hard to understand, most often because they want the querent to think more deeply about the questions we have asked. So the lot caster has to be an active listener and take the role of intermediary, which is actually a very active role.

We could even say that our lot casters are not allowed to be merely a mouthpiece. Among their duties, besides active listening, is the responsibility of giving an accurate translation and interpretation of what the powers said, which requires active participation and often considerable energy expenditure.

Our teachers used to say that the lot casters are half of the lot casting process.

Which brings us back to the necessity for competency, character, ethics, and a genuine link with the powers, all of which help to get effective answers, accurate messages, or successful healing.

Our literary tradition indicates that when powers gift one with "opening eyes"—that is, make one into a seer—we can tell the gift is really genuine because it includes a number of facets:

- The gift of asking with clarity

- The gift of hearing the message from power(s)

- The gift of understanding the message

- The gift of correctly interpreting the message for the asker

- The gift of then conveying the message ethically (with respect and accuracy) to the querent in such a way that the querent understands

These gifts deserve further discussion.

Asking with clarity: We often find that there is more than one question embedded in what the querent asks. Or, because the problem is complicated, the querent is confused about it, so they have trouble asking a focused question.

It is the job of the lot caster to work with them and to help them clarify.

The powers need this a lot less than we do: Perfect language is not needed, but some clarity helps the querent and the seer to better understand the answer. When in doubt it is best to say only: "I wish to hear what I need to hear."

Hearing the answer: It may seem unnecessary to say this, but just as the lot caster is supposed to pay great attention to what the querent means to ask, it is equally important to pay deep attention to the answer you receive. The response can be misunderstood, even by somebody with a great deal of lot-casting experience.

Understanding the message: It must be remembered that lots operate as a sort of telephone from the metaphysical powers to the lot caster. The lot caster must interpret and relay the message. Powers may offer subtle answers or deliberately obscure ones, presumably so that the querent will think things through. Powers sometimes simply respond with a picture or simile consistent with the cultural context of lots.

Let's say an answer involves camels, but the person asking has seen those only in the zoo, so that imagery is of little help. This is where the cultural knowledge of the lot caster comes in handy.

Sometimes, when the answers are blunt, the asker will think them too brief to address their complex issue. But there often is greater depth to be found. The experienced lot caster can help to clarify.

Correctly interpreting the message: This can be tricky. The lot caster must develop the skill of filling in the "blank spaces" of the sometimes terse or simple answers that Hebrew lots so often bring from the Otherworld(s).

It is also important for the lot caster not to allow preconceptions or even prejudices to color the interpretation of the replies. The same applies to bias or prejudice toward the asker. We cannot correctly interpret if our personal feelings cloud the issue.

Conveying the message ethically and with accuracy: Being self-aware is vitally important for good lot work. We think it is unethical not to be monitoring how we feel after a fatiguing day. If the connection to the liminal spaces and powers is impaired, the seer is denied clarity of vision and cannot report back properly.

It needs to be said that a diviner can become overloaded, then tired, and, in the long run, even burn out. Some—fortunately only a few—become jaded; they listen with only half an ear and not with their heart, let alone with their soul, which is what houses the gifts of seeing.

This is true in other helping professions, too; the person experiences compassion fatigue, is not aware of it, and start to blunder.

Another type of situation that can really challenge a lot caster is when the querant asks hard questions about "life and limb" issues. This is perhaps the area of operations that can cause the ethical seer the most heartburn. It is not usually difficult for a diviner to operate ethically and with reasonable accuracy when the question being asked—while of great importance to the querent—is not one of life and limb. But when life-and-death questions are being brought to the lot caster, it is another situation entirely.

In real life, the solution to a life-and-death problem may not be one of making good decisions versus bad decisions. In reality in the case of life-and-limb situations, our choices can range from a horrible option to a ghastly one. An example would be the asker needing to decide whether to take a loved one off a respirator at the end stage of life.

Hearing people asking questions when facing such issues can be truly difficult for the lot caster.

One may not smile and pretend that the answer they got is all unicorns and rainbows and roses. This is where, of all things, neither a lot caster's connection to the numinous nor any great metaphysical gift plays the decisive role. Here, what plays the most important role is character: the level to which the lot caster has kept her or his humanity and compassion. Yet this must be balanced by a lot caster's obligation to give honest answers. Simple but not easy.

One wouldn't think so, but what is sorely needed in this type of situation are good social and conversational skills. For example: One young quadriplegic asked a seer to ask the lots, "Will I ever walk again?"

The lot caster (a very experienced seer) saw in the lots that the energy in the answer, while not unmistakably so, very strongly tended toward "No." It was not, however, definite. The asker, moreover, was young and strong, plus medical knowledge can improve over time. In such a situation, saying "no" would have deprived the person of hope; whereas saying "yes" would have given them hope that might have been unjustified. What was clear was that the lots had not given a firm answer.

What to do? The lot caster, after reflection, truthfully said: "This seer is not given a clear answer."

In our judgement, this was the ethical way to respond.

When lot casting, it is permissible to recuse ourselves from answering. In which case, we prefer to suggest that the querent see another seer whose integrity and competency we trust.

This course of action is preferable by far to failure to walk the path of ethics, which can cause even the superbly gifted to no longer be the proper vehicle for relaying messages from the Otherworld. The powers disapprove of unethical behavior, and the seer's clarity will be impaired, whether the lot caster is aware of this or not.

This tradition in no way implies that the lot caster is expected to be some sort of saintly, perfect human being. Still, they should act ethically. Before continuing, here is what the tribal ethics requirements of AMHA traditionally are.

Peaceful Warrior Values for the Lot User

COURAGE

Practice a life of courage. Never be an accomplice through inaction.

Comment: In ancient days, that referred primarily to physical courage. We know today that moral courage is just as important—sometimes even more so.

HONOR

Behave honorably—to yourself and to others. In fights, do not sully your sword.

Comment: This has a lot to do with acting in seemly ways; refraining from pettiness. So we must avoid malicious glee; avoid lording it over those who have less power than we have and are vulnerable to us. We also need to learn to honor the self, which can be a difficult task if we were raised in a culture that promotes feeling guilt.

Regarding the sword, this refers to ethics: No spiritual and peaceful warrior is allowed to "beat those who are already down," or their sword (their honor) is sullied; that is, it is a shameful act that will result in withdrawal of favor from the powers.

HOSPITALITY

Practice hospitality and follow its rules; remember, a guest in your house becomes a guest-friend. Therefore, be choosy. Do not dispense your guest friendship lightly.

Comment: In older cultures, people who have been guests may well become friends made for life and there are assumptions, to various degrees, of mutual support.

FRANKNESS

Say what you mean. Mean what you say.

Comment: It is very important to learn how to do this with consideration and skill.

FRIENDSHIP

Sworn friendship mutually commits. Do not swear friendship lightly.

MODERATION

For your body: no intoxication; moderation in food and drink. For your soul: have passion, not fanaticism. Live for a cause rather than kill for it.

Comment: This is self-explanatory. It also means to not be intolerant in matters of politics or religion.

SIMPLICITY

KISS: Keep It Simple, Stupid. Don't clutter your life.

Comment: It is also of value to keep one's emotions and relationships simple and uncluttered.

GENEROSITY

Be big hearted: generous of mind, of heart, and with resources. Refrain from pettiness.

Comment: We are our siblings' keepers.

STEADFASTNESS

It is unseemly to be fickle. Keep contracts and commitments. If you cannot do it, say so frankly and renegotiate. Stand by your friends. Stay on course.

Comment: This should not be mistaken for stubbornly clinging to a path if it is proving to be unproductive. If a contract or commitment no longer works, we need to renegotiate, not simply suffer through it or quit without explanation.

INTERDEPENDENCE

Live in symbiosis with others. Value the strength of more than one arm, the richness of cooperating minds. Know how to offer help. Know how to ask for it.

Comment: Knowing how to ask for help is particularly hard for people raised in "rugged independence"–loving cultures. We humans are primates, and primates are social animals. We need our privacy, but we also need to understand that we need one another.

AUTONOMY

Stand tall. Earn right livelihood. Fend for yourself.

Comment: And think for yourself, too.

FAMILY

Give family its due respect, blood kin or sworn kin (kin of choice).

Comment: We only live this life once, and time goes by very quickly. It is all too easy in the busy Western world to have no time for family. But family of blood or choice is like a tree that needs to be periodically watered; that is, the relationships have to be cultivated to do well.

Even if we cannot love our family, or some people in it, we can still practice civility. Keeping a civil tongue in one's mouth is important. Walking away from painful conflict is sometimes the only option.

We know of somebody who so hated his father that he refused to bury him. We know of another who started a furious argument at the viewing of his mother's body. We believe that there is no obligation to *love*, but one should always act with respect. One does not need to love or forgive to act with civility.

What Questions Can We Address with Lot Casting?

If you are the lot caster, discourage questions whose answers can be found by consulting the phonebook, or on the Internet, or in a doctor, lawyer, or psychotherapist's office. Tell the querents to consult the appropriate human experts for such questions.

Asking the winning numbers for the lotto or what color shoes the querent's friend was wearing yesterday are insolently meant, and the caster should make that point if this occurs.

All other questions pertaining to one's life choices or situation are acceptable.

Some Caveats for Lot Casters and Askers

We need to clearly tell our querents not to blindly follow instructions from the lots. If major decisions are at stake, we have them consult another lot caster or other suitable divination expert before making any major decision.

If we are lot casters, we need to remember not to cast lots or use them for other magic if we are impaired. If we have a cold or are otherwise unwell, or if our judgment is affected by emotions, or if we have taken mood-altering drugs, we must refrain from doing readings. Under no circumstances cast lots, or do any other ritual from our tradition, while intoxicated.

Nor should we cast lots for a querent who is impaired or, perhaps, has a mental illness. We are not qualified to assess the possible impact or ramifications of a reading. For example, we may not be able to understand the impact our words may have on them and may thus do damage. Even when reading for the seemingly mentally unimpaired, we must be circumspect as to how we voice our readings, because words can cause harm. This is simply ethical practice.

We do not cast for somebody who is on the verge of committing violence to others or to themselves and who seeks our sanction for that.

It is important not to be tempted to cast lots or do any other magic with minors. I will not to do any lot magic with a minor who says, "Oh, my parent says it is okay." I will always check with the parent or guardian first. Ideally, the parent should be asked to actually be present. However, if parent cannot be present but gives their consent, then lot casting or other magic is permissible.

Self-Care and Other Ethical Obligations for the Lot Caster

As mentioned, casting lots or using lots for magic and healing can be draining. We are accessing the liminal and serve the powers and the community. While not a passive tool, we are still a tool of the powers when casting. Even the smartest and most sentient tools must be well maintained.

So take care of yourself. Being able to access the liminal spaces does not make us invulnerable or invincible. In fact, great receptiveness, if a caster is not trained well, can result in excessive vulnerability.

Also, we need to remember that casting lots is a service to a person or a community of persons. Done to aggrandize ourselves or to impress others is an offense to the powers and the ancestors.

When we operate as a lot caster, the querent trusts us. Their trust is a gift to us. It is vital that we never abuse that. While their trust and openness to use may increase our ability to help them, it also increases their vulnerability to us. Abusing the authority that being their lot caster confers on us offends the godforms.

If we are tempted to control a person toward whom we feel anger or disapproval by casting lots for them then skewing the answers, we are perverting the purpose of lot use and violating the mandates to offer our best and most honest interpretation or magic to benefit the querent. Anger and negative emotions cloud our perspective and our vision, and casting lots when we are thus impaired is a misuse of lots and thus an offense to the gods.

Because it is important to remain as objective as possible when reading lots, it is also best to avoid casting lots for ourselves or for people we are close to. Small questions are okay. Important ones are definitely not a good idea.

There is that saying: "Be careful what you wish for." When we ask a question of powers, we may well get an answer.

So if our querent's question is a momentous one, we need to ask them if they are sure they wish to hear an answer. If they say yes, it is no longer our place to judge whether they should ask the question. We must be considerate, but we must not sweeten or censor the answers. It is our obligation to use enough social skill to be able to pass on the lot message accurately and in the clearest, most beneficial way for the querent. If we think our social or communication skills are not up to it, we develop them—or we do *not* cast lots for others.

Sometimes, in rare cases, the powers' answers feel flat or dead, or their meaning is almost dramatically cryptic and cannot be interpreted. It may be a signal to the caster to not continue questioning in that direction. If our connection to the spirits is sound, we will know when to keep silent. It is appropriate to say simply, "I am not given an answer for you."

To summarize:

1. We must not give answers to make ourselves look good, knowledgeable, or important. Lot casting is not for self-aggrandizement. We need to stay on top of our human desire to impress others. This desire is universal and not wrong, per se, but it can put a seer on a slippery slope.

2. We do not cast lots for minors, guide them in meditation, nor do magics with them without their parents' or guardian's consent. Parents or guardians of a minor should be present at the casting unless they specifically choose not to be present.

3. Examples of inappropriate questions are: "Will I win the lotto?" or "Do I have cancer?" The first is not a question for lot casters, because any future we predict will cause it to change; this is almost a law of nature. The second, because this is a question for a doctor not a seer.

4. If we have to simplify language to get the message across (for example, for somebody less educated than we are or somebody equally well educated but who does not speak the language well), then we need to be respectful. We are *never* allowed to talk down to our querent. We are in service to them, not they to our ego.

If we do not know how to avoid talking down to
those whom we may think less fortunate than ourselves,
then we need to either learn how or refrain from casting
lots for them.

Lots are a simple and powerful tool, with its roots in tribal shamanism. First, we must look for their simplest, most concrete interpretation and avoid flights of fancy or embellishments.

When the querent asks a question, make sure you understand not only the words but also the intent and meaning behind them. The lots will answer those "hidden" meanings, and if you have not caught on, you will miss the answer's import. It will confuse you and the querent.

We may be lot casters; powers may have gifted us with the ability to meet them and hear their answers; yet we are still fallible humans. We are all prone to ethical missteps. Ethics is not about not having shortcomings; ethics is about acknowledging our limitations, honoring them, and working around them. This is important when reading lots or when doing any other kind of lot magic. It will make a better, clearer reading and better magic; this benefits us and the querent.

9

Meditation and Magic

Lots and Meditation

There are many different ideas about meditation. Some religious groups think of praying and meditating as the same thing. Or that to meditate, one has to do it in one traditional way and/or be a follower of a given faith. This is not the AMHA position.

There are some methods—inspired, I believe, by some ancient and venerable Eastern disciplines—that maintain that meditation consists of completely emptying the mind. For others, the ultimate goal is to reach connection or even fusion with infinite. In AMHA, empty minds are not our traditional goal—with or without lots.

Meditating with lots can have a variety of purposes, such as getting "in sync" with lots and what they can do. One of our preferred methods, used by beginners and experienced lot users, is the twenty-two-day meditation. This is not as daunting as it may sound. It consists of meditating on one lot for a half hour or an hour every day. That is, on day one, start with the first letter, Aleph, and meditate on it. The next day, do the same with Bet, and so on until the last letter is reached. We recommend not straying from the order if engaging in this practice, since there are overlapping meanings that are lost if one picks the lots randomly.

Beginners find this technique especially beneficial because it helps deepen the understanding of the lots and builds and strengthens their energetic connection to them.

Preparing oneself to meditate with lots is much the same as preparing oneself for casting lots, which has been described earlier. It includes going to a quiet space and anointing oneself or using a candle or other light. Take out the lot you plan to do the meditation with, read the lot poem that summarizes its meaning, then allow your mind to reach a state of deep calm. Even experienced lot users will, from time to time, go through this twenty-two-day lot meditation, because it keeps the energetic connection clear and sharp.

Some practitioners prefer to do the twenty-two-day lot meditation at night. They put the lot they are working with under their pillow and use it as an aid for lucid dreaming.

Whether for practice, for deepening the connection to lot energy, or for developing a discipline of calming the mind and aiding reflection, this is a most beneficial spiritual practice.

One can also use lot meditation to address a particular issue in one's life, a practice we prefer to recommend to people who are no longer at the early learning stage. Preferably, this should be used by people who have done the twenty-two-day lot mediation at least twice, and who have been practicing the use of lots long enough to know the key meaning of each lot mostly by heart and without need to refer to the book. In this method, rather than meditating on all twenty-two lots as described above, the practitioner can select a lot whose aspects are most closely related to the issues they need to work on.

For example, we may believe we have a difficult boss. Now a boss can be perceived as difficult because they are; or perhaps they are, but the problem is made worse by our own issues with authority, which may go back a long time before we met this boss.

We may or may not know which it is. Either way, Aleph (the chieftain) would seem to be a good choice for meditation. Once that determination is made, and after selecting the lot we wish to work with, we recite the relevant lot poem to focus the intention.

Then we proceed to meditate on that lot. One session may not be enough; it may be necessary to work on that lot each day, or at night with the lot under the pillow, for a week or even longer. This is the only type of situation in which we recommend just picking one lot to meditate on, rather than doing the twenty-two-day cycle. Continue the meditation practice with the one specific lot until things begin to resolve or answers are forthcoming.

Some people have reported meditating on one specific lot for as long as thirty days, roughly one lunar month, because the issue they were working on turned out to be difficult to sort out. We discourage meditating with any one letter for any longer than that; mostly, it is not necessary and sometimes can even be counterproductive because mental or emotional fatigue sets in and the meditations lose their effectiveness. In which case, it is the fatigue rather than the difficulty of the issue that becomes the problem or adds to it. One's brain may start going in circles, and there may be more effort than results. It is fine to abandon the issue for a while. The brain needs its rest, and mind and soul need to percolate what the meditation(s) brought up.

Often, after having taken such a break, people find that another, different lot should be their next step. For example, in the case of the difficult boss, after working with Aleph, maybe one needs to start on Lamed, to learn how to cope.

Which lot to use for meditation Workings can be difficult to identify sometimes, so we advise the beginner to consult with an ethical and experienced practitioner before trying to engage with a lot themselves; a mentor can help with choosing lots appropriate to the situation.

Besides, even if we are experienced, it is good to have support. We do not hesitate to use a "good ground" crew by asking one or more capable and trusted persons to act as mentors and guides.

Whichever lot meditation method we choose, whether we are beginners or more advanced, we need to remember that using lots is a magic Working; we cannot say often enough that focusing ritual intent, gathering will, clarifying intention, and chanting the relevant lot poem before beginning are crucial steps.

The short poems set down for each lot have layered meanings whose energy is captured within, which is why we recite them first. Chanting or speaking the lot poem helps choose which aspects of the lot to work with. It is good practice to use the poems in this way regardless of what level of proficiency we have reached.

Some examples of meditation topics are offered following the description of each letter, beginning on page 83. These are outlines only. If the reader chooses to use some of the examples we have set down, they will need to adjust them to their need, flesh them out, and give them further structure.

If you do not feel able to design your own, don't. There are reputable teachers and mentors you can ask for guidance. Just make sure you choose ethical ones.

About Lot Meditation Journeys

People from many different spiritual traditions have many styles of meditations, each with different purposes and differing depths of the meditative state. The same is true for AMHA lot meditations. In general, the most commonly practiced meditations by people in the West, regardless of whether or not they are on a specific spiritual path, are the well-known guided meditations. They are most frequently used for people who are beginning trance work and are usually led by a trusted guide who does the narrations and monitors the trancer's state of being.

Some people record what the guide (counselor or mentor or shaman) said while narrating the journey so that they can later play back the narrated journey as needed. Trance journeys can also be entirely self-guided. Self-guided meditation is easier for people who have more experience or for people who are good at self-starting, but many, even experienced trancers, simply do not like to self-guide and prefer to work with a guide.

Either way, we AMHA often affectionately call the both methods "shamanic tourism" because it seems that you are asked to not immerse too deeply but instead "stay in the bus," keep your arms inside the ride, and do not stray from the guide's path—in other words, the idea is to take no risks so that you won't get emotionally hurt as you go through the Otherworld landscape. Sometimes we also call them R&R meditations, not only because they require light trance and no great experience but also because their main purpose is to have a pleasant calming and grounding effect. So people typically go to favorite Otherworld safe places, such as remembered or imaginary beach or a restful copse of trees; they may swim with dolphins under the sea, or chat with unicorns or deer, or have tea with their favorite auntie . . .

Some people sneer at such "light" work.

It is very important to know that we AMHA do not in any way use "shamanic tourism" or "R&R journey" as a derogatory term. At a minimum, guided or unguided meditations of this "light" type serve a purpose that psychologists and clinical hypnotherapists correctly call "ego strengthening"; that is, the practice clarifies and grounds both soul and mind and enhances self-regard and self-esteem. These meditations can also help with anxiety. All this is extremely beneficial. Practiced regularly, the R&R journey can change people's lives for the better.

There also are some more advanced (complex) techniques. They may derive from the remotest times of shamanic practices, and we often refer to them simply as "deep journeys" or "shamanistic journeys" (as opposed to shamanic).

Shamanistic journeys are self-designed and self-guided. They involve states of deep meditation during which physical movement becomes difficult; yet one has to be able to control the proceedings that doing deep work in deep in trance entails and to return oneself to present reality when done.

AMHA is not a tradition with many types of complex nomenclature; so we use the terms "shamanistic" or "deep journey" fairly casually. They refer to two different types of deep meditation.

The first one refers to meditative journeys, usually employed for a quest for self-knowledge or better inner clarity or for a variety of other reasons.

The second one refers to a practice that occurs over a number of meditation events, and it is a series of meditations in pursuit of a specific goal, usually self-healing or deconstruction of trauma that affects our here and now. So we also call these by names

such as "long-range journey" or "long-range reconnaissance"—
or even, jocularly, " long-range monster hunt."

These terms makes sense to the AMHA, since in Israel, all
people—men and women—have to serve in the military, and
AMHA has its roots in Israeli culture. While not all people serve
in actual combat, everyone has a sense of what the hardships
are and how harrowing military reconnaissance, often behind
enemy lines, can be. These kinds of reconnaissance journeys can
be daunting. At a minimum, they are hard. They require a good
deal of mental stamina and groundedness, so they are unsuitable
for people who have just begun a practice to find themselves or
to become more rooted and stable. Experience and good deal of
mental sturdiness are needed.

This "journeying" technique has been successfully used by
combat veterans who need to detoxify from the damage their
war experiences have caused them. It can be used successfully
by victims of other types of trauma, as well.

As one would before a wilderness trek, or a reconnaissance, one
has to be well equipped. Knowing what one is trying to achieve,
setting a goal (the purpose of the journey) but being ready to reach
it in stages—over a day, week, or even months of practicing the
trance state—is key. One has to be willing to a go a long distance,
know when to stop to rest, reach for successive milestones until
one has found the otherworld place were the "monsters" lurk. I
know of people who have persisted over months or even a year or
two until the goal was reached. This regimen consists of very deep
and courageous self-work. It is not suited to all meditation practitioners, even if they have a lot of experience with altered states.

Like a real-life long-range patrol or a hunt, the long-range
journey practitioners go deep into themselves, looking for
"monsters" to neutralize, such as traumatic memories or events

and the issues arising from them. This practice requires self-discipline, a sound journey methodology, and, frankly, good nerves. Some refer to it as a type of "psychic self-surgery," and it is a procedure only for more advanced meditators who have achieved a great measure of control and self-discipline—not only because the practitioner reaches very deep trance states and pursues weighty issues but also because without the proper techniques and experience, one can actually incur in additional self-traumatization and emotional damage. For work like that we highly recommend accessing a reputable and knowledgeable spiritual mentor, preferably with pastoral or clinical experience in the field of trauma resolution. For this reason, we will not describe in detail how this is done.

For this type of Working, a lot can be used, chosen to operate either as an anchor or, better yet, a compass to keep one on track as one repeatedly proceeds across the Otherworld landscape toward the goal. It can also aid one's return to ordinary reality, which is not always easily done otherwise. As said, achieving the goal may take many sessions. For some, the lot is chosen to serve as a talisman (bringer of good) or as amulet (averter of bad). Or all of the above.

Otherworld Landscapes in Lot Meditation

I have mentioned a journey "landscape." Scholarship literature, such as Mircea Eliade's famous and seminal book *Shamanism: Archaic Techniques of Ecstasy*, shows us that in journeys of the shamanistic type, which is what the long-range journey is, the practitioner moves through a "culturally predetermined land-scape"; that is, one that is rooted in settings of traditionally handed-down, culturally determined mystical environments ("the Otherworld map").

Regardless of the specifics of any culture, what we call journeys have a couple points in common: There is usually a definite starting point, and there may be encounters or ordeals along the way. The long-range journey eventually leads to the Otherworld location where the traditional powers can be contacted, or where whichever goal one was after can be found. Sometimes, several smaller goals need to be reached as one progresses through the journey before one can attain the ultimate goal.

The mystical "landscapes" are products of handed-down culture and metaphysical heritage, so people belonging to a traditional grouping have an inbuilt consensus about what the place "looks like." Journeying through one's own traditional landscapes, therefore, yields the best results. Yes, it really helps to be raised with those internal maps, and moving around the Otherworld has often been described as being in familiar territory since there is a measure of cultural consensus as to what the landscape is.

But this is the modern world, so what do we do if we were raised in an industrialized Western nation; that is, if the culture our ancestors grew up in has lost the maps we would have called our own and where there are no more traditional teachers? Finding a suitable "landscape" to journey in when we do not belong to any one traditional/tribal culture requires a lot of learning and a lot of practice.

Some people adopt paths of ancient traditions, which in our view is legitimate only if done respectfully and with the full consent and approval of teachers from that tradition.

Failing that, many post-tribal, neo-shamanic methods have been designed in modern times to be culturally neutral so that modern people of any origin and background, for example, can use them to meet their needs. The reason all these methods can work is because the human brain is able to learn trance and its uses; also, due to our shared neurology, the stages of journeys are, at least in outline if not in detail, much the same.

Read, study, find a reputable and ethical teacher. Properly taught and properly learned, modern adaptations can work as well as traditional ones.

We lot casters, of course, have our own traditional landscapes, the products of our history and culture. Unavoidably, the landscapes are Mediterranean brush country, as in northern Israel, or arid steppe/desert, as in the south. Alternatively, there are oases. Abodes, if found, will usually be mud brick or stone or tents. The animals inhabiting such landscapes are the ones that exist—or existed—in the physical landscape today: camels, ibexes, gazelles, wild dogs, onagers, jackals, lions, domestic goats and sheep, and any other animals of those areas, past and present.

It is not in our tradition to call upon animal spirit helpers or guides when we engage in our journeys. But our culture, as any other, attributes certain characteristics to certain animals—the donkey is strong, the lion is ferocious, and so on. So their appearance may convey some meaning, and they will, on occasion, show up. One cannot be sure they will, but if they do, they will be consistent with the culture. We have met warrior angels (our culture has no "cute" ones), ancestor spirits (always benevolent), or ancestors who have been gone so long that their faces and individualities have been forgotten, so they have blended back into nature as talking trees or talking animals (frequently birds).

In learning to use lots, even for lighter forms of meditation, we become acquainted with the metaphysical landscapes and their inhabitants. This is why so much time has been spent talking about our values and culture, and why we recommend you take note of your own while you study the use of lots.

It is good to practice achieving altered states until Other-world travel comes smoothly. Once it does, our traditions teach, we believe that we are ready to use lots in meditation journeys and, with the appropriate training (and if necessary), for long-range journeys that lead us to deep healing.

Some Observations about Magic with Lots

We are a sloppy lot, unlike practitioners of ceremonial magic, so we use the word "magic" interchangeably with the words "energy work," "spell," "incantation," "blessing," and so forth.

Lot magic is *always* benevolent magic. Lots are never to be used to curse someone. That type of magic certainly exists (and is even practiced by some ultra-orthodox Kabbalists during a full moon), but it is our belief that since curses send toxins out—and we are the vehicle through which the magic flows—curses should not be associated with any lot use. So while blessings and healings are freely discussed in this book, curse magic will not be.

As with lot meditation, lot magic usually involves the selection of one or more specific aspects of the lot chosen for the Working. The magical act will involve coalescing that lot energy and project-ing it in the form of a spell for beneficial blessing or healing or as empowering magic to help ourselves or others in need.

For example, one might use Gimel as a healing spell to ease a person's fear of going on, say, an airplane trip. Or one can use He to call upon godforms and ask them to benevolently watch over a person.

Using Lot Magic with Respect

A few caveats about using any of the lots for magic.

1. We never use a magic ritual, no matter how beneficial and no matter how seriously we think a person would benefit, without the recipient's explicit permission. Just because they know us does not make it okay.

2. Even if the recipient allowed it once, we still must ask for permission the next time and each successive time.

    The only exception to rules 1 and 2 is if the person is unconscious and cannot give permission, but either has asked for this ritual in the past or is known to have a spiritual tradition that would accept it.

3. Our loved ones also need to give us specific permission.

4. For any blessing magic used for minors, we get the parent or guardian's permission and have them present, if possible.

5. We make sure to tell the person that we are helping that blessing magic is no substitute for medical or legal guidance; for that, they should call a doctor or lawyer.

6. We make it a firm rule to never touch the person for whom we are doing blessing magic unless it is absolutely necessary. Most often, it is not. If we think we must, then we make sure to ask permission and make sure the touching is not sexually suggestive in any way. In many cases, it may be preferable to have somebody else present to act as "chaperone."

    Also, it is crucially important to remember that some people may be too shy to tell us if touch makes them uncomfortable, so when in doubt, we don't. Disregarding this is a violation of their personhood, whether they themselves are aware of it at that moment or not.

People assume that the exception to this is when doing magic for our own partner or spouse. This is incorrect. When doing magic, explicit permission must always be given. We may make an exception only with our own, very young child.

If we break those rules, we are not only committing what we call a trespass—which, being a violation of boundaries, is a breach of ethics—we are also invalidating the positive energy we were intending to send. The blessing will go awry, missing its mark, because trespassing upon a person neutralizes magic.

We also need to make clear to people ahead of time that performing any kind of lot magic for anyone is, to us, a ritual. Even if it lasts only a few minutes and the setting is informal.

An Outline of a Lot Magic Ritual

If we are doing lot magic for somebody, we like to share what we are doing, either before starting or at each step, depending on what is needed. It is good for the process to be as transparent as possible.

Usually, as with all lot Workings, we prefer to start by anointing ourselves with oil or lighting incense (if the person permits; some have allergies to scents). If neither of these options is practical, we use one of those small, battery-operated "candles" to light the ceremony. We check with the client first, then our choice of which step to follow depends not only on which style of Working we are most familiar and comfortable with, but also on what the other person is fine with.

Always start the spoken part of this lot ceremony by formally asking the person for permission, even if they are the one who originally asked us to do it. It is actually part of the ritual to ask for consent.

We usually say something like: "It is our custom to ask for permission, so that you may open your soul's gate to the blessings and magic you have asked for and allow them to enter. Do you consent to this ritual?"

Or, more simply, "Do I have your permission to give you the energy of lot magic?"

They should answer with, "Yes I give you my permission."

This applies to *any* energy work on others, not only to spells with lots.

We will then take from its pouch or box the lot chosen for the Working. Preferably, it is taken with our dominant hand. We touch it to our forehead and heart, then just hold it. If the person we are helping is okay with it, we can ask them to lie down on a comfortable surface they can easily get up from. We let them relax and breathe deeply, then invite them to open to the energy.

If they don't know us well or feel too vulnerable to lie down for any reason and prefer to stand, we explain that we will gently surround them with the positive energy contained in the lot we will be working with. We always honor the wishes of the person we are performing the magic for, and we are not by tradition allowed to override objections.

If the person has a lot set of their own, and they agree, we can take the lot chosen from our set and have them hand us the same one from their lot set; we then hold them both in our dominant hand. Or, we can have them add our lot to theirs and hold both for a moment before returning one or more lots to us. This adds to the power. While chanting and without touching them, we pass the lots over their body from head to toe, doing circular motions. Tracing the lot in the air or above the person is also a choice; they can request that we not do it.

If they are standing, we walk around them three times, chanting or speaking the lot poem and our own addition if there is one. We will know if it is necessary for them to add their voice to ours as we chant the incantation. If they do not know the words, we can do it with a call and response technique. Our metaphysical intuition will guide us on how to proceed.

If needed, and we are both comfortable with it—after first asking permission—we can clasp hands with them and hold the lots between our touching palms, then walk a circle together three times. Unlike in some European traditions, there is no positive or negative association to the direction in which we circle. Instead, we move as the Working energy requires.

We use the terms "sunrise" or "moonrise," rather than *deasil* or *widdershins*—which may be more familiar to Western Pagans. Sunrise, like deasil, refers to the sunwise or clockwise direction. Moonrise, like widdershins, means to take a course opposite the apparent motion of the sun as viewed from the Northern Hemisphere.

People often ask us what words to use when performing lot magic. We build a lot spell by first reciting or chanting the lot poems specific to the letter(s) we are using. Since lots have a variety of layered meaning, the ritualist performing the magic will need to mentally focus on a meaning that is relevant to the reason for which the magic is being done. We have some traditional chants, but what melody to use is truly up to us. However, since this is about magic, focused intent and will are not optional.

If more than the initial chant is required to raise the right energy, we can repeat it; it is also traditional to improvise words of appropriate incantations. A few frequently used traditional examples are given in the next section.

We also use ancient magical formulas verbatim, but do so sparingly. Some of the incantations we use with lots can be traced as far back as ancient Mesopotamia, and there are similar ones in other parts of the ancient Middle East. Many of the spells we use today have developed over time.

One reason for not adopting ancient formulas indiscriminately is their wording. Whether spoken in ancient Hebrew or in translation (which often fails to capture the essential energy of the words), ancient words do not always work well with modern people's language, imagery, or sensibilities. For a formula to work at its best, the person for whom one is doing the spell needs to be open to accepting its full meaning—since they are partners in the ritual. Lacking an understanding of the language causes a kind of energetic incompatibility and as such can impair effectiveness.

We will offer some traditional verses here and there—some of which are very ancient, some less so. Those of us who are agnostics and do not follow any of the powers can use all of the verses set down here, with or without addressing a specific power, just by changing the words accordingly. Magic with lots is a ritual in and of itself; it will work as long as there is respect for it, we know how to focus will and intention, and the words we have added to the spell do not contradict what the chosen lots actually mean.

These ritual procedures will help to optimize the effect of magic Workings with lots.

10

The Lots

The Meanings of the Letters

Over the centuries, many sources—including the rabbinical ones—have offered different meanings for each of the letters. This is, in part, colored by ideology. We cannot deny that in the AMHA tradition, this is the case as well. We try for authenticity, but thousands of years have gone by, so the way we read lots today is greatly influenced by information from modern secular scholarship as well as evolving tradition.

Cultural assumptions inevitably color how we read lots, and the culture is rooted in the land where lot casting started. Each letter has an associated poem that contains some—but not all—of the key meanings of the lot. Without understanding those aspects, proper communication between the seer and the powers will be problematic. It would be like trying to communicate while speaking different languages.

The following discussions of the lots contain meditations and magic rituals that can be used to deepen your understanding of the lots and/or to help others. Even is not specifically stated, each meditation or ritual should be begun by holding the lot and reciting or chanting the lot poem.

1

א

Aleph

Chieftain, bull, one thousand (meaning "many"), abundance or riches,
strength and empowerment

Aleph the chieftain
One thousand and wealth
Great Bull of Heaven
Old God who is kind.

Aleph (also spelled Alef), as all the lots discussed, has a number of meanings, or aspects. Before it became a letter, it was the stylized sketch of a bull's head. Indeed, Aleph sometimes refers to the bull—which was a symbol of grizzled El, father of all our gods, also known as El the Kind by ancient Canaanites and early Hebrews.

Aleph also meant the number one thousand (so today the lot's meaning is also "many" or "much"). It also was used to symbolize a herd of one thousand cattle: This was a huge number of cattle in ancient times, so today it can mean riches or abundance. Aleph also meant "leader of one thousand," a designation that ancient Hebrews used for a battle chief or a chieftain. In the modern Israeli military, Aleph has still been used to designate the field leader of a troop of any size.

Aleph most frequently means "chieftain energy," and that this energy is currently playing a role in our life or that it should. Lots can be blunt. Sometimes (but rarely), Aleph may mean "put on your grown-up pants" and deal more decisively with your situations (as a chieftain would).

Usually, the lot Aleph tells us that in the situation we are asking about, "chieftain energy" plays a positive or negative role. This can help us look at the situation more closely. The power of Aleph can come from a variety of people: those who have formal authority over us, like a boss at work, or those who informally have such a role in our private sphere, like a parental figure, an older friend whose counsel we deeply trust, a mentor, or teacher. Aleph may also refer to our own authority over others.

Sometimes, it is a warning against abusive authority—our own or somebody else's. Or perhaps the querent has difficulties dealing with authority, and Aleph may tell them that they need to work to get better at that. Since our issues with authority are often caused by past events, this interpretation is not uncommon. Maybe we are still wounded from an unpleasant encounter; or maybe we did not have the chance to learn the type of social skills needed for dealing with authority. In these instances, the lot is telling us that authority energy is not only active but also that we need to touch our own inner power to better cope with it. Perhaps, like a good chieftain, we need to manage our own responses or those of others with more tact and skill. As the saying goes—and we value this saying in AMHA—"true strength is delicate."

Many people are so triggered by persons in authority that they fail to learn to deal with authority effectively—or with their own responses to it. So an alert from Aleph can mean "learn how," which, of course, can come in handy. But we have also seen situations in which Aleph essentially meant "go get another job; this boss is hopeless, and you cannot fix him or her, so fix the situation by walking away." This meaning would not come from Aleph alone but also from the other lots in the cast.

Aleph most often encourages us to examine our own personal empowerment (or lack thereof) and how, consequently, somebody else's power (which can be positive or not) currently affects us.

It may tell us to connect to our own inner chieftain. Or perhaps, instead, we need to moderate how we express control over others.

Now, those of us who like history know that in real life, chieftains could be nasty people—cold, harsh, and even cynical individuals whose human kindness may not have extended beyond those they commanded, if even to them, and who showed little or no consideration for those outside their circle. This is not the meaning that Aleph necessarily has in lot casting, unless it is to warn us about our own failings as authority figures or that we need to watch out for the destructive authority of somebody else.

Instead, Aleph is an idealized chieftain's power of respectful and benevolent strength. Indeed, "get in touch with your inner chieftain" most often means "find your strength, tap into your inner resources," so it is one of the more helpful suggestions brought to us by Aleph.

These meanings are the ones we most frequently encounter when casting Aleph.

But, as mentioned, Aleph also means "one thousand," which used to mean "many" or "much," as in one thousand men or one thousand heads of cattle, and therefore implies abundance or riches.

This does not necessarily mean that your querent is going to win the lotto. (For one, as discussed earlier, lots are not predictive of events, only of where patterns may lead.) Instead, "riches" most often refers to a sense of abundance, emotional or spiritual, which is a lot less dependent on getting rich and a lot more on one's emotional position toward life. The rest of the lots in a casting, complemented by the energy-reading skill of the seer, tells us which of these aspects of Aleph the lots are addressing.

Two Meditations with Aleph

If we are guiding somebody else's Aleph (or any other lot meditation), we start—as with all rituals and lot magic—by formally asking the other person's permission to do so. Obviously, if we are not guiding, we can skip this step. Compose the mind for meditation, hold the lot in your hand, and chant the lot poem for Aleph.

This simple act is a very powerful vehicle to call to ourselves that aspect of the lot's energy we wish to focus our will and intention upon. It is also useful for boosting your energy level, especially if you are depressed, or very tired after a long day, or not feeling well. (If those feelings are severe, refrain from using lots until you feel better.)

If you are facing an unexpected promotion and are intimidated by taking on a leading role at work—a situation we encounter frequently when people ask us for lot work on their behalf—doing a Working with Aleph is helpful. It can bring good results and a change in your attitude, thus leading to better responses to the word around you.

Choose which of the aspects of Aleph you wish to meditate on.

Chant the lot poem for Aleph and hold the lot in your hand or over your heart.

Set your intention, focus your will, and take calming breaths. Now visualize this scene:

You are walking on a desert plain. The sun is high and pleasantly warm—not yet hot—and the air is dry and smells of the sage and wild thyme that grow along path you are on. Your walk is comfortable; you hear the faint crunch of sand and pebbles beneath your sandaled feet. You come over a gentle rise and see ahead of you—a little uphill from where you are—the place that you are seeking.

It is a green oasis, a circle of tall, beautiful palm trees the color of emerald against the bright tan of the surrounding desert. You smell the breeze coming gently from there, the scent of green things and of water. There will be welcoming shade and comfortable rest on fallen palm fronds.

You begin walking up the gentle slope, then the path angles gently down. You follow it down and down, further and further, closer and closer to the oasis. Then you reach it, and you walk amidst the lovely shade of the great trees, the slender trunks reaching for the cobalt sky above; you hear the gentle clatter of palm fronds in the breeze. You go in further, and you smell water; as you get closer, you hear gurgling, the welcome sound of the small, sacred water source that gives these trees their life. You stoop to drink; the water is clear and clean and when you straighten up again, you follow the small stream further in, to the oasis's center.

There, in a small clearing, the water forms a pool. You see a being sitting beside the pool—the chieftain, weapons laid aside, seated comfortably on a rock and leaning back against a palm trunk. You stop to look at the friendly, sunburned face, creased with laughter lines and lines of maturity and wisdom; you feel the strength and kindness and great power and gentleness. There is a staff in the chieftain's sun-browned hand; a beckoning gesture invites you to come closer, and you notice a comfortable stool beside the seated chieftain. You approach, you sit, and there you ask your questions: questions requiring answers, questions requiring advice, questions requiring encouragement—whichever of these you need, the chieftain will patiently reply and meet your need. Or maybe even tell you that you must come back to get more answers.

When you are done, you bow your head in thanks, rise, and turn away. You retrace your steps, cross the oasis, and make your way back along the path to ordinary reality, knowing that you can always return. The chieftain will always be there, offering counsel and support and strength.

A Magic with Aleph

All lots can be used for talismanic magic (which brings good energy in) or for averting magic (to block undesirable energy). Whether you are doing the magic for yourself or somebody else, the procedure is mostly the same.

Start with reciting the lot poem. Since you are using the lot as a talisman, chant or speak the lot poem for Aleph while holding the lot in your hand or over your heart. The melody or cadence does not matter. Find your own. Invent one; hum it or tone it. Do whatever feels right to you.

If you are doing this magic for somebody else, you can ask them to lie down; walk around them three times, chanting. (The same may be done if they remain standing.) After chanting the Aleph lot poem, if you feel the need, you can add:

> *Find El's power to be loving*
> *Find El's power to be strong*

Find El's power to heal gently
Find El's power to understand

This is obviously a favorite for those who are devotees of El, but you can omit the deity's name if you prefer; that is:

Find my power to be loving
et cetera

We have found that this spell, used both before and after a meditation on Aleph, or even on its own, is an effective Working.

If used as talismanic magic, it works well for pregnant women who want to attract strength, health, and abundance into their baby's life. In that case, the power and strength of Aleph as the bull symbol is wanted, as is its aspect of abundance. Use those as your intention for the blessing spell.

Averting Magic with Aleph

If there is an authority figure we have a concern about, for example, we can use the Aleph lot for amulet magic, to keep bad chieftain energy at bay. A helpful side effect is that it often strengthens our own inner chieftain at the same time, so we can more comfortably and kindly deal with the issues bad chieftain energy causes for us. This use of the lot as amulet can help avert a potentially bad situation from getting worse.

Even just holding the letter Aleph and chanting the lot poem daily, or for as long as a person feels the need, has been shown to be helpful.

2

ב

Bet

House, home, family, ancestors, lineage, bloodline

Bet is for household,
Your ancestors' line,
All of your kin—those
You are born to stand by.

Lots when cast, rather than simply giving us answers, sometimes hold up a mirror to us and tell us about our present life or way of being, thus helping us to understand ourselves and how we live our lives. The letter Bet is a good example of this. Bet is related to the Hebrew word *beyt,* בית (house), as in home, family, lineage, or ancestry; the people in the place or community where one's roots are. This can also be what people in the West call "family of choice," but those links have to be deep and of long standing, and the term does not apply to "here today, gone tomorrow" relationships. In other cultures, anthropologists call them "fictive kin"; that is, people who are playing the role of family members and are accepted as such but who are not blood related.

Some American communities have such relationships as a matter of course—aunties or uncles who are not related to the family but are regarded as such and are involved in the family's life. If they are departed from this plane of existence, they may also fulfill the role of ancestor for the querent and so show up as Bet.

Bet never refers to people we like but have just met, no matter how exciting their potential for deepening a relationship may seem. We hold that close relationships require time and, like trees, plenty of watering to grow. Bet sometimes also represents the place—usually metaphorical—where the querent can at last find the spiritual home that they may have been seeking.

This leads to another meaning of Bet: ancestry. Ancestors are a particularly strong energy present in Bet. In our tradition, and in many other traditional societies, the concept of having ancestry—a community going back in time, in addition to the one in the present—makes us part of a greater whole. Ancestry can bring a sense of belonging, and it therefore forms an important component of identity, which can help to develop a stronger sense of self.

Bet in a casting frequently refers to deceased family members, who may be present during the casting or in the person's life. They may just show up in the casting because they wish to be remembered. What can come through in that case is a sense of, "You never call, you never write."

A comment we often hear is, "But how is this possible? I don't know my ancestors. I don't even know the name of my grandparents, so how does lot casting or meditation or magic with ancestors even pertain to me?" The answer to that is that you may not know your ancestors—but they know you. Those among us who do not know their ancestors may still have objects on their ancestor altars to symbolize the unknown elders.

Being conscious of one's ancestry, or even one's connection to still-living older members of our family, is an element of personal identity that Western society has weakened. I still remember a speech during somebody's college graduation. Several of the most successful students were giving speeches for the occasion. A young man, looking very much like the proverbial future leader of a corporation, was first.

He walked to the mike and gave a good speech. It was filled with youthful cockiness and self-confidence, filled with phrases such as: "I am proud of my achievements. I have worked really hard. I have taken initiatives. I have not given up. I have always reached for goals. I have never stopped reaching, striving to go higher, to be stronger, better, faster." A young hero, battling on a mountaintop, alone except for the obstacles to overcome. If some corporate recruiter had been in the crowd, the boy might have struck him as exactly the type of person suitable for hiring and advancement—a sure candidate for a successful career.

The young man who came next stepped to the podium, and the first words out of his mouth were, "I want to first of all thank my grandmothers and my mother, who encouraged me to go to school and to not give up. They believed in me, said that I would do well in school. They were the ones who worked hard so that I would only have to get one job while going to school and could study better. Anything I have achieved, I would not have achieved without them."

This attitude—recognition of the value of belonging, of the strength one gains from a true community rich in social support—is a value reflected in Bet, and other lots as well.

Ancestors also bring good counsel. While in some populations, there is a folkloric belief in malevolent ancestor spirits, in AMHA, we hold that no matter how nasty Aunt Sally may have been in this life, once she has become an ancestor by passing to the Otherworld, all the toxins of the present life are gone. As your ancestor, she must have your back, be truthful to you, be protective, and stand by you. So in lot Workings, we can trust ancestors as advisors, protectors, and benevolent entities. The only "negative" things they can do to us is not show up when we'd like them to or just be unwilling to answer a question.

If ancestors show up in a lot casting, offerings of remembrance—water or wine or food—help solidify the link to the ancestral line, thus solidifying our identity. Tightening the bond with one's ancestry aids in the ability to withstand adversity or hardship, makes us feel stronger as individuals, and fosters greater readiness for cooperation and mutual support. All across the lots, you will see the implication that interdependence makes one strong.

By contrast, the typical Western society highly values "rugged individualism." Like all societies, it "markets" concepts of how one is to be. A sense of community or link to ancestry is almost lost in the industrialized West and perhaps in the USA most, barring some communities of color and some small-town communities. "Rugged individualism" has a lot of positives; it definitely has its place, since it leaves ample room for personal development. But like most—if not all—human social constructs, it can be taken too far. When this happens, it impairs the health and well-being of people's hearts and souls. It can cause a sense of loneliness or pointlessness or void in an individual's life and a disorienting lack of a grounded identity.

For example, we have found that when Bet shows up in a casting, sometimes its energy moves us to ask the person how many casual social contacts they have per day outside of work. To which they frequently answer with blank looks. Or they find, on thinking about it, that they can count the number of nonwork social contacts on one hand. By contrast, more traditional peoples "have people," and this is where Bet can hold up a mirror. It can help some realize that they don't "have people," that they feel a void, and that they attempt to fill it with substitutes: by working harder, to the point of being too busy to stop and feel; or by making shopping their main source of pleasure; or overeating;

or turning on a screen and binge watching, after coming home to an empty house, in an attempt to drown out the silence. Such people often dread retirement because they have too little to do, nothing to fill the space that work used to fill.

Thus, in alternative spirituality communities, we find many who go on quests to "Find out who I am" or "Find myself." Their discomfort comes not knowing their place in their human ecology. Bet may point them to the fact that they have this need and that they would do well to attend to it by becoming active in seeking and finding their "home."

You do not find people in more traditional, community-oriented societies saying, "I don't know where I belong" or "I have to find myself." They usually know who they are.

When society determines that a way of being is the "only" way to be, it also often decides that the opposite is a fault or weakness. Rugged individualism can foster a deep fear of dependency. It blurs the difference between dependency and interdependence. This can cause a fear of befriending people, because that would require taking on obligations toward them and expecting whatever support is due from the type of relationship, or fear of interacting more with kin who, for whatever reason, one knows one cannot love. Bet in a lot casting often also uncovers this dilemma.

We think that having friends or kin and loving them is a blessing, but having kin we cannot love does not mean that we are evil. The culture that the lots are rooted in holds that kinship "obligations" only oblige us to act toward them in a civil and decent manner but no more.

Bet in a casting can refer to any, or all, such issues.

A Meditation with Bet

The whole topic of Bet—home, family, ancestry—can be a painful one for many. Maybe there have been losses in the family, and we still miss the counsel of our elders. Or perhaps we want to learn how to improve relationships with those of our lineage who are in the here and now. Have we had issues with family members at events? How do we prevent them from recurring and turning into open conflict? Or did we perhaps have a family member who was frequently ill and could not have our back when we were growing up, and we still feel wounded even after they have died? These, and many more, are frequently the types of questions that we can address in meditating with Bet.

Take the lot Bet and hold it. Recite or chant the lot poem. Choose to meditate on any of the sample questions above. Or perhaps all you want to do is to reconnect with departed ancestors, known and unknown.

Imagine this scene:

> *Start walking through a landscape. It may be the one that the ancestor you are seeking connection with would have lived in long ago or it might be the landscape that you lived in with them while they were alive. Take the path; you cannot go wrong. Feel the gentle wind; the ancestor's voice calls on the wind. Follow the sound.*
>
> *The landscape will change. The sky is perhaps the fine blue of a sunny day, the temperature just right; there may be bright sun or a gentle light. It may change to the dark immense beauty of a star-studded night. Just walk along, listen to the wind, and follow the sound. You are holding the letter Bet in your hand, or it is perhaps in a pocket, so you cannot get lost, and you'll find your way to the ancestor and back.*

You reach a clearing, and the ancestor you are seeking is there. Take your time to look at the face, the demeanor, the welcoming smile. You have brought a flower and perhaps a jug of water or wine as a gift to honor them. Sit down at their feet. If you have questions, ask them. Or simply have a friendly chat and get better acquainted.

When you are ready to go, thank the ancestor for their time, or the counsel, and for being willing to be part of your life. Promise another gift of a flower, of water or wine, when you are back in the ordinary world. Then visualize yourself putting your hand in your pocket where the lot Bet is so that it will guide you back home to the present. It will take you back to the ancestor whenever you feel the need.

A Magic with Bet

Like many of the other lots, Bet has a multitude of facets, or layered meanings. So, as with other lots, there are a multitude of magics that one can perform for a variety of purposes, but they all revolve around ancestry, family, and home. We encourage respectful creativity when doing lot magic. Here is one example of how the lot Bet was used recently for magic.

A woman had recently lost her adoptive parents. She was debating whether to find her birth parent(s). She felt both hope and dread. "Will I like them? Will they like me? Will they be okay people? If they are not good people, what does that say about who I am? Do I want to even find out? Am I betraying my adoptive parents who loved me and raised me?" This last concern was strong.

There were five of us lot casters with her that day, and after discussing it with her, we agreed that Bet was the best lot to use to magic her main concerns—the first being to honor her adoptive parents' role in her life, the other to gain acceptance from her long-lost blood kin.

For this magic, three lot sets were used, since three letter Bet were needed for the spell. (If no additional lot sets are available, one can draw the letter Bet on stones or mark them on wood and either anoint them with incense oil or speak a consecration spell over them.)

We asked the woman to lie down (it was on a blanket under a tree, surrounded by summer grass) and hold a Bet lot against her heart. Four of us were the ritualists, two representing the adoptive parents and two the birth parents. The fifth person, being the shophet, was the main ritualist—but a shophet is not necessary for any of the lot magics described in this book (except for the ritual we call "Seeing for the Tribes").

The main ritualist introduced the "parents" to her with the simple words: "These are your birth parents. These are your adoptive parents."

The "birth parents," while holding hands, started walking around the woman, with the lot Bet held between their clasped palms. While walking, they chanted the lot poem for Bet. The "adoptive parents" did the same thing, following closely in the "birth parent's" footsteps and joining in the chanted lot poem for Bet.

Meanwhile, the main ritualist asked the woman to breathe peacefully and raise the hand holding the Bet lot, keeping her upper arm resting on the grass but lifting the lower arm from the elbow, and keeping the lot in her gently closed fist.

Then, while walking around her still chanting, all four people in turn touched their clasped hand with the lot Bet in it to her raised fist that also held Bet. They repeated this, circling until each of them had been around her three times and had touched her hand with the letter Bet three times. They then stopped in a circle around her.

Then came the spell closing formula: "May the power of Bet bring light and warmth to your endeavor. Selah."

Normally, this would have been the end of the spell, calling Bet energy to the woman, her departed adoptive parents, and to her encounter with the birth parents. But because of her very high level of unease at the thought of the step she was taking, the main ritualist stepped in and added another spell. This was optional and most often is not needed. The ritualist speaks a verse, the querent repeats:

Ancestors, ancestors, of soul but not blood
who took me in your heart
who raised me to love you,
Before your souls crossed

I long knew your love
I still know your love

and you'll always have mine.

I now need your blessing
to seek blood and bone
My father who made me

My mother who shaped me
while still in her womb

I owe them my life
I wished them to love me
but they had to leave

I wished them to love me
but they had to go.

By blood and by bone,
By heart and by soul
by Bet and its power
may they open their arms.
Selah.

We then asked her to hold her own lot Bet to her heart with both her hands, thanking the adoptive parents for all they had done for her, and taking ownership of the magic we had woven with her.

She said later that during the spellwork, she felt a warmth come over her, which surrounded and embraced her. The lot Bet gave her strength and approval from her adoptive parents; as she reflected on the ritual later, she knew that it had helped her feel that, regardless of what her birth parents might be like, just knowing that she had them and meeting them finally would be enough. If it turned out that they were unable or unwilling to relate to her in life, they would be able to when their turn came to move to on to the next plane. The woman later told us that she had eventually met them, and they now had an ongoing, warm relationship.

3

ג

Gimel

Travel, movement, transportation, metaphysical journey

Gimel the camel
A journey you face

Go into Farland
In spirit to grow

The name of the letter is related to the word *gamal,* גמל (camel). In desert countries, camels served most of the functions of a horse, except for plowing.

Camels were ridden; hence, Gimel means "travel." Camels made long, hard journeys across desert or semidesert possible. They were able to carry heavy loads for long stretches and did not need water, as other beasts of burden did. Hence, their association with long travel rather than short trips.

In the concrete here and now, the letter Gimel in a lot casting could indicate an impending physical move or the need for one. Moving to another department, or a new job, or away from or to a relationship, or changing the location of one's abode can also be signaled by Gimel.

In its metaphysical meaning, Gimel can also mean travel as a "journey" in the sense of a vision quest, shamanic journey, or even the whole process of personal, spiritual, or metaphysical journeying that we call the long-range journey. Gimel may be telling the querent to engage in a meditation practice, or to engage on a spiritual path, or to resume one if they have neglected it.

As always, the specific meaning of a lot will be clarified by the other lots in the cast.

Camels have a heaving kind of step, which can make some people mildly seasick or give them a backache; so finding Gimel in a casting also reminds us that the camel ride ahead of us, or that we already are on, may not be entirely comfortable. This is true whether the "journey" is a change in the here and now— such as a new job, new living quarters, or new relationship—or changes caused by meditation or by the practice of the long-range journey.

If a person finds Gimel in a casting, and they already know what the "journey" is that they should or will be or are undertaking, they may know at least a little of what impending changes are likely to happen. Meditation on Gimel can be useful for sharpening their insight and helping them to be better prepared.

A Meditation with Gimel

This meditation can help with the unease of movement or change in one's life. Take the lot Gimel and hold it. Recite or chant the lot poem. Then imagine this scene:

You are in a beautiful desert landscape. Around you are reds and tans and browns, a richness of color and rocks of many shapes. The air is warm and dry and smells of sun and sand. You have slipped into a reverie, and your eyes are closed.

You can feel the heaving step of the camel beneath you. Perhaps you notice now that the journey is long, and you are beginning to feel a little uncomfortable sitting high on that camel, knowing that there is such a long road still ahead.

But you know that Gimel, the camel, leads to a desired destination . . . and can adjust to that which is new on your path. As you think of that, your camel's step seems to become softer, to heave less, and your sense of discomfort decreases.

There is a destination ahead, and it will be good to reach it. When you remind yourself of that, you begin to look forward to the camel ride still ahead.

A Magic with Gimel

Here is a spell that we use for blessing a person's impending travel—on foot, by car, or by plane.

Hold the lot Gimel in your hand, palms outstretched toward the person you are doing the Working for, and recite or chant the lot poem for Gimel. Then say:

May your travels be easy
May the road be wide and rise to meet you as you go
May your camel's step be gentle
May the thorns of the Acacia tree turn inward as you pass.
And when you get home, may those who love you wait for you
with open arms.
Selah

This same blessing (with a different focus of will and intent, of course) a can also be used to help someone who is dying or who has just died, to ease their way as they cross over to another plane of existence to join their ancestors.

4

ד

Dalet

Gate, doorway, threshold

Dalet is gate to the
Places beyond

Stand at its edge
Or cross to the other side

Dalet sounds a lot like the modern Hebrew word *delet*, דלת, which means door or, more specifically, a threshold.

Thresholds in ancient Israel had significant spiritual and legal meaning. In the Jerusalem Temple, doors separated the public spaces from the spaces accessible only to the priests. And in the towns or cities, some ritual and religious rules and laws are applied very differently if one is in the inner (private) sphere or in the outer (public) one.

Therefore, Dalet in a lot casting signals that we are currently standing at a threshold. If we cross, it will change us from one way of being to another. This is something that one may prefer not to think about; people sometimes dislike being on the verge.

Sometimes, we do not know that we are facing a threshold in our life until Dalet's presence in the cast helps us acknowledge it. We may feel pressured to make a decision to cross, or to refrain from crossing. Perhaps we already know there is a choice, but we simply have not decided what to do. A threshold of this kind can cause various degrees of emotional, psychological, or spiritual stress.

The message from Dalet very clearly does not blame us for that stress, certainly not if crossing the threshold means making a difficult decision, one that may bring momentous change. Lots do not blame; they simply point out . . .

The meaning of Dalet is not limited to showing us a demarcation line between ritual space and daily space, or the "here" and the "there," or the sphere of people and the sphere of spirit—though it can mean any of those.

It means we are facing a choice—we can make it or not. We can opt to stay right where we are. At its most concrete, Dalet can simply mean that we may choose whether to get a new apartment or look for a new job. Stepping over the threshold can mean accepting or refusing new responsibilities, moving out of one's parents' home to go to work or school, go from living alone to sharing space with somebody else, or starting or ending a relationship.

Still, while Dalet may point to changes in ordinary life, the ensuing change can be a major one. We once saw Dalet show up in a casting when the querent was debating whether to step away from working in a corporation to start training to be a healer. Dalet appeared in a casting when a Bedouin youth of our acquaintance was seriously considering accepting a scholarship, which would have moved him away from his tribe and a semi-nomadic herder lifestyle to settling down in one place with strangers.

Another time, Dalet showed up as we were casting for a woman from India, who felt called by a godform in the Hindu tradition but who was facing the decision of whether to accept the call and become a follower of this godform or to stick with the godforms of her family tradition. So Dalet can indicate a spiritual shift taking place if you cross, or choose not to.

Dalet does not pressure us to move but shows that options exist right in front of us. It does gently hint that making the choice would be the best path, but this is by no means a command. This is often when the querent needs to be reminded that there usually are more than two solutions to a problem, that there are more options available than we think. Making a decision, when standing at a threshold, can sometimes take some courage.

It helps to know that crossing that threshold and going through a door is not always an unchangeable step. Learning will come from having stepped over the threshold and gone through the door. If one turns around and tries to go back out, which can often be done, the fact of having taken that step across the threshold cannot be erased. The experience will leave its mark (often positive) on the person and on their process.

Crossing, or choosing not to, might bring about exciting events and/or emotional or spiritual changes of substantial value.

One can even choose to remain where one stands. If the querent chooses not to make a move at all—neither crossing nor moving away, which Dalet sometimes indicates simply by showing up—our tradition considers that, itself, a type of choice. Events that the person might have had influence on had they decided which way to move may unfold differently.

So not crossing, not deciding, is in itself a choice.

Very, *very* rarely, and only in conjunction with the other lots in the cast, Dalet may be a definite warning of potentially negative change—as in, "Do not step across that threshold into that room." If that is the meaning, the other lots will make it abundantly clear. A warning of this type is never a nuanced statement and almost never occurs.

On a different topic entirely, Dalet can indicate that a person whom we know is dying is getting ready to cross. This should not be read as prediction of death for somebody who is not actually, medically known to be about to die.

A Meditation with Dalet

Since Dalet represents a threshold and/or a door, people have found it helpful to use the following imagery, or imagery of a similar type.

It is an ancient evening. Sunsets are fast here, and stars are beginning to show in the sky, which has been rapidly shifting colors from the day's cobalt blue to the first tints of pink, flaming red, and orange.

You are standing, clad in sandals and your linen robe, your cloak thrown over your shoulder against the cool of the rising evening wind.

Before you is the oaken door of a finely made mud-brick building. The door hangs from its leather hinges, and it is ajar. The soft glow of oil lamps from deep within almost reaches you; there is just enough light for you to see the threshold, which is a little high and cut from fine stone. It may be easy to stumble over it in this half darkness.

You have a decision to make: if you cross it and enter, new rules, the rules of the house, will apply to you. The lifestyle within, its chores and its joys and its duties, will become yours. All you have to do is cross and not trip.

You are not sure what you want to do. You could turn around and leave, but what would you miss if you do not go in? And what would you miss if you left?

So you stand there, unable to decide. Some people step past you and go in. Others come out. Which will you be? The one who goes in and commits or the one who stays out and leaves? Then it occurs to you: You don't have to decide at this moment. You don't know enough about the situation; you need to know more. You can wait until daytime, until the sun shines and throws light on the house so that you can see it better, so that it casts more light on the issues, and until you've asked more questions, until you know more.

Once you have learned enough about what going in would mean, you can come back and make your decision—go inside or close the door from outside without going in.

And if, when you return, you make the wrong choice—be it leaving again or finally stepping over the threshold inside—you can retrace your steps or leave by the back door. You can always reverse course. No decision, save one of life and death, is ever final.

With this knowledge, you can go off to think. When the sun shines on the world and your vision is clear, you can sit under your favorite tree and ponder some more, until you know what your choices will be.

A Magic with Dalet

Go through your usual steps of burning incense or using a scent, or light candles, real or battery operated. Hold the lot Dalet in your hand while focusing intent and will for the magic. If you are performing the incantation for another, follow this by asking them to hold their Dalet, if they have a lot set, while you hold yours.

If a specific power has been enlisted to help, it is best to thank them by giving them a small symbolic gift—a libation of wine, beer, or water; a small morsel of tasty food; a flower . . .

Speak or chant the lot poem for Dalet. Tell the person for whom you are doing the spell to repeat each line of the following incantation.

I look at that threshold
I look at the change

I see what's behind me
not sure what's ahead

With ancestors' blessings, decide if to cross.
With ancestors' blessings, I am ready
I'll be ready to choose.
Selah

5

ה

He

Any godform, numinous energy, spirit, divine being(s),
the infinite (*Ayn Sof*)

He is for Spirit
In all its great forms
Soul of your Soul
And the Wise Ones That Know

The letter He in a casting signals the presence of, or influence of, one or more godforms or numinous powers in the life situation the querent wants to ask about. The letter He translates as "spirit," so its meaning is not limited to godforms in the Canaanite/Hebrew pantheon. It describes instead whatever is experienced and believed to be numinous. This word comes from the Latin *numen* (divine will or power), denoting therefore the energy or emanation or presence of beings that are sacred.

We often use the word "godform" or "numinous" when explaining He in a lot casting, because in our AMHA tradition, anybody of any faith or spiritual tradition may cast lots or have their lots cast for them. Thus the letter He refers to "spirit" as each individual understands it.

In our AMHA tradition, all the sacred powers of our pantheon are called the "elohim," a masculine plural of the word "el," which is not a name but means a god. The personal name El also means God but is the name of the Father God (known also as "El Elohim"), because he is the God of (our other) gods.

By contrast, the letter He, standing for all our elohim as well as for godforms of other beliefs, is "nondenominational" and embraces a broad range of meanings. In our culture, long after tribal traditions, He was used in literary tradition to refer to God (the god El, who later became conflated with Yahweh); later still, in medieval times, He was translated as אֵין סוֹף (Ayn Sof), that which is infinite, unfathomable, spirit transcending even godforms, a vast and pure high entity in its broadest, most transcendent form—so transcendent that it cannot be fully defined.

This meaning rarely occurs in a casting for a devotee of our traditional elohim, since it is not consistent with (neo) tribal culture and is more suited to the scholastic mystic.

For all these reasons, when the letter He is in a casting, both querent and lot caster may not be able to identify which godform's energy is manifesting. In our tradition, that is not a matter of concern.

Sometimes, a querent may ask a fairly pedestrian question—about work or everyday life issues—and, startlingly, He shows up in the answer. The querent may be surprised that mystical/spiritual energy is involved in a question that they thought was only about something simple. But, then, spirit is in everything and everywhere . . .

A Meditation with He

Given the broad meaning of the letter He, personal beliefs in given godforms will most likely determine how to use this lot in meditation.

People report meditating on He in a variety of ways. As with other lots, if they want the lot's energy to affect their life in some way, meditating on it daily or sleeping with the lot for longer or shorter periods of time are techniques that are effective.

People have asked whether to meditate on He for a full lunar month, since that is done with other lots. However, with He, this approach is used only by people who wish to start being of special service to their community, by following—or as we say, becoming a devotee of—a specific godform that He represents for them. This means engaging in a more closely personal relationship with their He.

Some people (mostly those culturally influenced by monotheists faiths) ask us for lot casting because they want to know which godform is calling them and/or if they should become a devotee of that godform. Others ask lots how to better understand the role a given godform may currently be playing their life. Some people meditate on He as a way to deepen their understanding of one, or all, godform(s) and how to relate to it or to them.

Sunlight. You find yourself on a gentle hillside on a path that is filled with light. You know why you are there, and you know what you are seeking. You know it deep in your bones, even though you may not have words for it. What you want is to touch the energy of the power with whom you wish to connect in your meditation.

You begin walking on the path. You feel numinous energy, and it gently grows in you, around you; as you go, you feel that, yes, it is calling to you. You follow it, in trust and in love. You cannot get lost; you know how to follow the call; you know where it leads you. As you walk along the path, the gentle breeze keeps you comfortable, despite the sunshine. You smell the scent of the flowers that are dotting this beautiful landscape and breathe it in deeply. You stop to drink from a small clear brook running beside the path, and the smell of flowers is in the clear, cool water.

The path dips very gradually, and you go down, gently down, further down. Now you can see your destination, the top of a gentle hill a short distance from where you are. There, on the flat top, is a grove; you can see the crowns of its great trees. It is a sacred place, a High Place, and there the godform that you are seeking, the godform that seeks you, resides. As you go on a little further, you begin to see between the leaves the stela which is set in the grove to honor He.

The most sacred of trees, the terebinth oak, is there before you, its wide branches shading the High Place from the sun. Like a guardian, it protects the small stone altar that you know is set there for the power you are seeking.

Your breath comes evenly and easy as you crest the gentle rise. From beneath the sheltering shade, you can now see a warm glow, a light. That light is there for you; it is there to welcome you; it is He that has come here to meet you, and it is just as you have wished. The power appears gentle and safe, so you know that it is fine to go closer and to sit on the sun-warmed stone bench that faces the altar. There are flowers on the altar and a goblet of wine and one of water for libations.

He shows itself and speaks. You see its face and its shape—or maybe you just see a vague smoky outline—and you sense the energy that comforts you, as you had wished. And you know in your soul, in your bones, that here is your shelter and your protection and that He can help find comfort and answers. And, among the many things you hear today, is the welcome news that you can return here whenever you need.

A Magic with He

In working magic with He, because we use its name or that
or any of our elohim, what we are really doing is asking them
directly for a blessing and protection.

One of the most ancient blessing spells—reputed to be the
remnant of the oldest blessing in the Hebrew literature—asks
for the help of the blended feminine and masculine numinous
energies. This is a powerful blessing spell, not to be used lightly.

This is my own translation of this blessing from the Hebrew
Bible, *Bereshit* (Genesis 49:25), and it is adapted to AMHA polytheist beliefs:

By the elohim your ancestors loved
By the elohim who loved your elders
I bless you with the blessings of the Heavens above
I bless you with the blessings of the Depths that are below
Blessings of the breast
and of the womb.

Selah

6

ו

Vav

Peg, hook

Vav is the peg from which
what is next hangs

Things you let hang there
Will hang there for long

Vav in a lot casting tells us that something in our life (presumably described by another lot in this cast) depends upon another thing (also presumably expressed by another lot in the same cast).

This could be an action that needs to be taken before another one can be a success. Or Vav can be saying that in our life (past or present) there is something that we are "stuck" on, and progress or resolution depends on our moving to "getting unstuck."

To understand Vav, it helps to imagine that a garment you are wearing got hung up on a peg protruding from the wall as you were intending to walk by, and it now prevents you from proceeding. You can continue on your way, but first you need to attend to the situation.

Vav can also help us to realize that we are stuck in the first place. Or it may signal a graver situation—telling us, for example, that we are solidly tethered, which effectively prevents us from currently moving at all. The analogy here would be to imagine a large tent that you want to dismantle and pack up, so you can leave. However, the tent remains solidly anchored to a peg stuck deep in the ground, which is very hard to remove and thus prevent you from moving on. We saw this meaning when casting for a woman who needed to leave an abusive husband but was prevented from doing so—paralyzed, in fact—by the deeply rooted notion in her own mind that still accepted her parents' opinion that the abuse was her own fault and that she should stay in the marriage and work harder at being a "better wife."

Vav almost always implies that we can, in fact, be freed from the peg by our own actions. The value of Vav in a casting is that it helps us to recognize that which impedes forward movement, but it also suggests that once we know this, we can take the appropriate steps to unhook ourselves.

A Meditation with Vav

As always, recite the lot poem first. If you know what you are "hung up" on, think of it and focus your will and intent on understanding why and finding solutions. If you do not know what the problem is, just focus on the visual of the peg and the sensation of being caught on it. Recite the lot poem a second time if you feel the need.

> *You are walking downhill. Down and down. You have walked for a long time, but you keep going. The sun is high overhead, hot on your back. The sun has bleached the dust path so much that in the bright light, it almost dazzles your eyes, interfering with your vision. You continue to walk, then at last you leave the path you have been on (it seems forever) and walk on golden summer grass toward a large round meadow.*
>
> *In the center of the meadow is a wide-crowned oak tree. This is a High Place and outdoor sanctuary, so there is a large, open*

well beside the tree, surrounded by a finely carved stone wall. You know that a few steps lead down to the water. You have been here before. The crown of the great tree you are approaching is so wide that it throws cooling shade over the well, offering welcome shelter from the sun in this summer that is hotter and drier than usual.

You have a large, empty, clay water jar on your shoulder that you are planning to fill. You set it down so that you can rest for a while first; the way here was long. You sit down in the shade by the trunk of the tree and rest your back against it. You see people coming and going; they have water jars, too. They go down the few steps, then come back up with jars slopping water on their shoulders. This is surely welcome, for it really is hot.

You know that you would like your own jar to be filled; you know you would like water to drip refreshingly on your shoulders as you hoist it up and start walking back; you know that you could get up and fill your jar at the well; but you really do not want to move, so that cooling water seems out of your reach.

The jar will be heavy once filled, the path will be long. But you really ought to do something. You wonder why you won't move. You half-heartedly try to get up, heaving a sigh. But you don't really mean it; besides, you find that the back of your robe has become entangled in something, preventing you from rising to your feet. Perhaps it is a low hanging branch or a snag in the bark of the tree or the thicket of nearby thorns. You do not know what is stopping you; you cannot see behind yourself well enough to be able to tell nor can you reach. If you try to simply rip it away, you may get scratched by thorns, and you also know that you will badly damage your clothes, a costly loss of a hand woven garment. Moreover, if you tear it, you will have to walk around with a torn robe that you will not be able to hold closed while carrying a full jar. It may leave you half naked, exposed . . .

So you sit back down.

This has happened before. You need to move but are stuck, and you are afraid to take action. Nothing new.

But wait, there is something new. This time it is different.

This time, as you try hard to figure out what to do, you crane your neck around farther than before. You can see clearly how your back got stuck. The tree is holding you fast, not the thicket of nasty thorns. The tree is holding you because it is trying to tell you something; this is progress, but you still cannot fathom how to get loose.

"Ask the tree what to do," a voice says . . . your own but not your own, a voice that is wise.

"Ask the tree," says the voice again. "It held you fast so you would ask what is stopping you."

Asking, really asking yourself that question is something you have dared not do, so have never truly tried before.

This time you ask the tree.

You lean back against its wide trunk, allow your mind to meld with the tree, and you find it is restful and safe; the living tree vibrant and welcoming. You feel the pulsing energy of the life in the tree, the flow of its sap.

You ask the tree without fear. This time you really want to know.

"How am I stuck, and how do I proceed?"

"I will tell you." The answers begin to come.

You listen in silence.

At last, you realize that it is not your garment that was caught by a branch of the tree, it is your soul that is caught on an issue in your here and your now—one that will not let you go until you have attended to it. You feel relief flooding through you, because there is a solution and indication of what you must do; it is not completely clear yet, but it is a good start.

You may have to come back here a few times to ask again, to understand more, and still more until it is clear. Or perhaps just one question is enough, and you will know.

For sacred trees, when consulted, speak only truth.

When you are ready to leave, just reach for the jar. You will find that it is full of fresh water. But somehow, when you carry it, it feels a lot lighter.

A Magic with Vav

Here is a spell we like for removing the "peg" or getting off it.

First, anoint with sacred oil if that is part of your practice. Or light a candle. Next, standing in a location you find suitable for this Working (before your meditation altar, beneath a revered tree, etc.), recite the lot poem for Vav to focus the intent and will.

Hold the lot Vav in cupped hands. Vav will be used in this magic both as a talisman (to bring a good outcome) and as an amulet (to avert the negative effect[s] of the peg). This spell works well to "jumpstart" the stuck person's progress.

Ancestors, ancestors, my voice in the Tree

come to my aid, show me my truth

*Show me the peg that my garment is
caught on
Show me the peg that I cannot see past*

show me the peg that is buried deep

show me the thing that hinders my soul

*Ancestors, ancestors, my voice in the Tree
help me remove it and
lend me your wisdom*

*Let your love guide me so I'll know my next moves
Let your love guide me so I shall be free.
Selah*

7

ז

Zayin

Sickle or weapon, also a warning of a potential fight

Zayin the sickle brings
Barley and joy

Zayin as weapon, defend
Your own field

Zayin, the sickle, was both a harvesting tool and, duly modified (made larger and heavier), it was used an ancient weapon. In archaeological excavations, at sites dating back to cave dwellers, sickles made of animal jawbones have been found. People would extract the teeth from the jaws and replace them with sharp flint or obsidian blades.

In the Bronze Age, they began making sickles of copper or bronze. At that time, so the story goes, the super-strong Hebrew war leader and seer (aka "judge") Samson was said to have used the jawbone of a donkey as his combat weapon. This is very likely an exaggeration, since if you've ever seen the jawbone of a donkey, it is a monstrously large item and would be very hard to wield, but it is in keeping with the idea that he was a type of ancient superhero.

Bronze sickles, being valuable, would have been passed down in families. Their later use as weapons is illustrated in some ancient Egyptian paintings—a kind of curved blade with a long handle that may have been their elongated version of a sickle, modified for war.

Today, except if you are actively in an actual combat zone, finding Zayin in a lot casting does not refer to a physical weapon such as a knife, sword, or firearm. Instead, it points to the fact that we are in possession of tools or "weapons" of a spiritual or emotional nature whose purpose is to bring us rightful harvest—such as right livelihood—or to be used by us to assure protection of our rights.

Therefore, in a lot casting, Zayin can either mean that you should reach for a "tool" (such as an action or series of actions) to begin "harvesting," or you need to brace yourself to use a tool intended for "war" or confrontation. Again, the meaning is spiritual. In no way does it mean that you should get a weapon and hurt somebody with it. It refers instead to taking a healthily assertive attitude. Zayin, we have found, often shows up when a person—too often a woman, alas, though certainly not always—has doubts about their right to make a good living. Or to ask for a raise. Or to stand firm.

So the first lesson of Zayin is that it is completely appropriate for us to earn right livelihood, to take steps to be fairly paid for our work, and to ask for the fruits of our labor without embarrassment or shame. It is okay to want and get a results from our labor—a "harvest," in other words.

As you will see in the sample meditation, Zayin can also mean that it is one's birthright to stand tall in life and stand one's ground. The cultural tradition of lots is that the elohim wish us to be assertive (but not aggressive).

It is all right to take steps that will bring us abundance, joy, fulfillment, et cetera. Even if people around us—or the voices living rent free in our head—tell us that it is not okay to assert ourselves. Zayin says that it is appropriate for us to stand up for our opinions, to speak up and speak out.

People are sometimes surprised to learn that the appearance of the sickle in a lot casting can apply not only to our relationship with humans but also, to some degree, to our relationship with godforms!

Many people, especially those who have been brought up in religions requiring unquestioning obedience to God or the gods fear that standing up to or questioning a godform is a sign of disobedience and that disobedience is "bad."

This is not so in the Hebrew tradition. The culture in which lot casting is rooted has a long tradition of "arguing" with powers. Abraham, as we see in the Bible, argued and bargained hard with his god over the issue of the destruction of Sodom. This is seen as positive, because he showed caring and concern for other humans. And there is even a story that when Yaakov (Jacob) remained behind, letting his people cross a river or wadi (dry riverbed), a godform—variously assumed by tradition to be an angel and/or the gods themselves—engaged Yaakov in an actual wrestling match, which earned Yaakov a dislocated hip but also his name Israel.

Being given a name by a power is, of course, an honor and a privilege, not a punishment. But it has its price, as is traditional in most shamanic initiations. So it derives from this that arguing over the various possible meaning of religious tradition, or arguing over decision that comes from a godform, is considered a good thing, because presumably one is trying to suggest a different course of action (like Abraham regarding Sodom) or to better understand whatever messages come from powers.

Godforms look upon us with favor if we stand tall, as we were meant to. From Yaakov's story, we learn that they reward us for "wrestling" with the gods, even though the process may be painful for us. This, by the way, also occurs in very ancient shamanistic traditions, where the shamanic initiation (which may include getting a new name, as in Jacob's case) can be paired with suffering.

There is a reading of Zayin that occurs more often if the querent is an AMHA member or the topic involves something concerning the group of AMHA. Since the standard (flag) of the tribe of Dan includes a sickle, Zayin can refer to an AMHA who was adopted into that tribe. Or Zayin can refer to a shophet. This is because the Dan, according to the archeologist Yigal Yadin, may not have been one of the original Hebrew tribes but became one of them over time. Their banners proudly displayed a sickle because this shophet symbol reminded all others that the "Dan will judge over Israel as though it were one of the tribes" (Genesis 49:16, my translation). This means that the Dan, too, could have a shophet arise from among their midst, which points to the inclusiveness of ancient Hebrew tribal society.

So sometimes, in a reading, the sickle Zayin may be a reminder of the importance of being inclusive.

A Meditation with Zayin

To further understand the energy of Zayin, let us try meditation imagery.

> You are farmer, living in ancient times. The late spring weather is hot and dry, as it always is, and, as always, it is a sunny day. You are working in a field of golden barley; you straighten up, wipe your brow, and take a quick break to drink from your goatskin water pouch before going back to harvesting the barley field's bounty with your bronze sickle.
>
> The field is yours, for it came to you as birthright from previous generations of mothers and fathers; the sickle, too, is yours

by birthright, having been handed down to you by your mothers' mothers. So you know deep in your bones, without even having to think about it, that doing what you're doing—harvesting in this field—is your birthright.

As you resume working—cutting the barley, bending over to tie it into sheafs, then straightening to carry it to your cart nearby—you see that there are people coming downhill. It is fine; being here and harvesting is something you have to neither ask permission for nor to apologize for.

But you're standing facing the sun, so you only see their outlines; their faces are in shadow, so you cannot quite tell if they are your friend or a foe. You stand up straight, you calmly let the hand with the sickle drop in a relaxed fashion along your body. You do not threaten, you do not shout or wave your sickle around. You simply stand tall. Your bones know that it is right for you to be here and harvest. No one can tell you not to.

You watch them come nearer—just wait, just hold your position.

They see you standing tall, so comfortably, holding your sharp sickle, quietly asserting your rights. If they are hostiles, they will see you would be too much trouble, and they will go elsewhere.

If, on the other hand, they are friendlies, they might say: "Oh, hello. Peace on you and yours. We see you are having a harvest. Our family just finished ours last night, and tonight we are having a harvesting feast. Would you and your people like to come celebrate with us?"

Either way, when they leave, you can continue to bring in your harvest.

A Magic with Zayin

Here is a spell that people find helpful. As with all incantations in this book, one can either use it to help another or chant it to oneself. As always, speak or chant the lot poem first. Use traditional frankincense or myrrh oil to anoint yourself, or use a candle or light, or burn incense before starting the Working. You may, as with all lots, repeat the poem if you feel the need to raise more focus or energy.

As is tradition, repeating the following incantation three times further helps raise focus, intention, and will, hence the power of the spell. Feel free to chant it more times if needed.

My sickle is sharp and
my sickle it bright

My Sickle's my birthright,
feels light in my hand

My sickle is my strength,
my Sickle brings bounty

It is mine to use
It is mine to have
From Ancestor's hands.
Selah

8
ח
Het

Fence boundary; risk of trespass, violation, offense

Het tells of trespass
Against your own kind

Violates the body, the soul
Or your mind

Het denotes a fence or a boundary marker that was or is or will be torn down or is at risk. Since ancient times, fences or walls delimit a person's or a family's property, and permission in some form must be given to cross that boundary. This is why, for example, we always ask for permission to use our energy on another for incantations.

While Het in a lot casting may point to a concrete risk of a breaking and entering of one's home, this reading only very rarely applies. Most often, Het signals that one's personal sphere is currently at risk for being invaded or "trespassed" upon or that it was trespassed upon in the past.

Het draws our attention to violation of a person's emotional and psychological boundary. Depending on what the other lots in the cast indicate, it can also mean that the querent, themselves, is at risk of committing—or already is committing—such a trespass. But it more often shows up when the querent is, or has been, in a relationship that involves a chronic pattern of trespasses and that the situation is (was) not healthy. It even refers to toxic relationships, like an overcontrolling partner or parental abuse of some kind.

If this is the case, the lot caster needs to be especially clear about which interpretation applies. In our experience, people (especially from the Anglo-Saxon world), when faced with Het, often assume that they have committed a trespass of some kind, that they are at fault for some type of violation of propriety, of norms or rules, thus offending or harming another person or even disobeying their god(s).

But we have found that in lot readings, Het far more often means the opposite: It is the querent whose personhood has been violated or abused, or is at risk of it. At a minimum, there are patterns of micro-aggressions from others. Het points our attention to something that may have gone unrecognized and that continued trespass has been or can be damaging or even is (was) crippling.

Trespass can come from various external sources—not only from family members but also from people with whom one is in a romantic relationship or people assumed to be friends who cloak their criticisms in fake humor. Less close to home, Het can refer to coworkers or superiors at work. Often, people who are treated poorly minimize it, so finding Het is an alert, a warning that can be of particular value to people who may have a history of being taken advantage of or being abused and whose ability to recognize this may have been blunted.

The appearance of Het can also tell us that we, ourselves, are the ones trespassing on our own boundaries; for example, by allowing bad behaviors against ourselves to continue. We may be experiencing emotional bullying or any other violation of our right to dignity. If the violations are severely unethical—such as elder or spousal abuse—Het reminds us that such acts offend the gods, that we are right to object to such treatment. We would say that the elohim expect us to respect others but also to respect ourselves. Violation of boundaries, or allowing violation of our own boundaries, is not, we think, what the ancestors or other elohim want for us.

That said, it is important to understand that Het is not in any way blaming a victim. It simply holds up a mirror. Alerts are not given if nothing can be done; so Het also says that there are means, even if not yet recognized, for putting a stop to such trespassing. If we are powerless because we were or are weaker than the trespasser, no fault nor shame lies with us. But as soon as possible, it is desirable to change that abusive power disparity—by walking away from it in whatever fashion and seeking help if one cannot do it alone.

There is no shame in seeking help. Het further implies that when there is damage from this trespass, one can practice self-healing to prevent us from further being a victim or perpetrator of trespasses.

A Meditation with Het

It may be surprising that people often need to see Het in a casting before they can become aware that trespasses are causing problems in their lives, or have in the past.

Given the severity of some types of trespass that Het can point to as causes of trauma, we do not offer here a guide to meditation on Het. Any meditation would have to be specifically tailored to the person and situation in question. It may be of value to engage in such meditations in close cooperation with a trusted teacher and competent mentor and/or work with a psychological counselor of some type who is willing to include and/or accept meditation on Het.

Speaking in generalities, because of how deep the issues of violation can go, a good practice when meditating with Het is to do it for minimum of a week. Discuss with the mentor or counselor what to meditate on.

Do you need to identify what the violations consist(ed) of? When and how do/did they happen? Are there moments that you can point to at which, realistically, you could have avoided what was happening? (The answer most often is no.) How do you heal from it?

With competent help, you can design appropriate Het healing meditations.

A Magic with Het

We have had victims of spousal abuse, as well as combat veterans, who have found this incantation most useful. These verses have been found to be effective at showing us how to protect ourselves from others if their actions can harm us in some way. It also is helpful if we, ourselves, are the ones committing the trespass, either against ourselves or others.

After setting up the space, begin chanting or speaking the lot poem for Het. Continue with:

Holy Lady who is All Mother (Ashera)
Holy Lady who is friend

By the Maiden who is fearless (Anat)
by the Maiden who wields Spears

Help me grow a sacred fence
Wolf or Hyena cannot cross

Help me see the living fences
I myself don't wish to cross
Selah

9

ט

Tet

Strange, alien, unaccustomed

Tet is for alien, for what I
Don't know
I have not been there
Feels too strange and new

Tet means strange, alien. Something I am not accustomed to. Something that "is not my flannel jammies." There may be something in our life that is new, or perhaps we have just noticed it, and we experience it as strange, unaccustomed, hence uncomfortable.

Tet does not in any way signal the presence of something seriously menacing or dangerous to life or limb. Instead, Tet merely says that there is a wobble in the existing equilibrium, either now or in the immediate future, and that this challenge will (or already does) push us out of our comfort zone. This can be a new person who has entered our sphere or any other situation that we either have not encountered before or that we only now, for some reason, find uncomfortable. Tet can also refer to unexpected changes in one's spiritual journey.

Tet does not allot blame because we feel uncomfortable. Lots do not blame. In our experience, this lack of blame often startles people who were raised in the West; they tend to think that feeling somewhat anxious or even fearful when faced with something new is at best embarrassing and at worst some sort of character defect.

In AMHA, feeling uncomfortable with the unusual is in no way a weakness. Rather, Tet simply points out to us that something unanticipated is going on; it teaches us that we should expect it and warns us that suppressing awareness of our own discomfort, rather than honoring it as normal reaction to change, often simply adds to the problem.

After all, concern about the unfamiliar must surely have been very helpful to our ancient ape ancestors. They would have been out of the gene pool if they had not known to be cautious and watchful when encountering something they did not know enough about. So don't let's think that feeling wobbly when faced with the unfamiliar is a sign of timidity or cowardice. Discomfort does not mean we cannot cope. Instead, Tet teaches us to accept the fact that we, as humans, are designed to feel concern about the unknown and that we can operate very effectively despite it.

Tet, in itself, does not determine whether the situation is positive or negative nor how it will resolve.

A Meditation with Tet

As always, feel free to adapt your meditation to more closely fit your own specific needs and/or consult with a teacher if needed.

You are about to enter a familiar place, a room that you have been to many times before—your sitting room, perhaps. You know the color of the drapes, the perfume of the flowers in your favorite vase; you know the softness and the texture of the cloth covering the upholstered chair you will be sitting on—everything is familiar and comfortable.

You chose the colors and the furnishings long ago. So long ago that you have been taking them for granted—the pictures on the wall, the carpet on the floor, the smell of the room from a bowl of potpourri with your preferred scent. This is how the room is supposed to be.

You step inside and sit down . . . but something is not right. Something has changed, and you aren't clear what it is. Is it the smell of the room? Or is the picture hanging slightly askew? Perhaps your favorite seat—the seat you have taken—is not as soft as before. Or has somebody moved it farther from the fireplace, far enough that you now know you will not be warm when you sit in the usual way? You cannot yet put your finger on what exactly changed the feeling, or perhaps you can—either way, you experience anxiety and discomfort.

Breathe deeper. Look around you. Try to discover what the changes are. Which ones cause you distress? Why are you distressed? Is there a fear of never again being as comfortable as you were before the change? Are you angry because somebody has come in and changed things around, so the space is no longer what you were used to and somebody else now controls what was yours? Perhaps you feel that you are powerless to change things back. Do you feel guilty about your own discomfort? What "bad" things does it say about you that you do not like change?

A figure appears, like a mist but human shaped, and you know it's your guardian, your companion. You hear a gentle whisper. "Shhh," it says. "Shhh," like a loving parent's gentle soothing.

In that sound, there are words: "Don't feel shame that these changes unsettle you, it's the way of things for most humans to startle when something is new. Have no fear. You can learn to move well in this space that has changed. You will not trip on the furniture that has been moved around, and you can learn to ignore the picture on the wall that you would never have hung there. It is inconvenient, but the discomfort will lessen with time. People can do well in uncharted lands. So can you."

And as the guardian whispers in reassurance, you begin to
feel calmer, then calmer still. You begin to see how to adapt and
feel well as you are learning to live with these new changes. Why
there may even be some lovely possible changes that you'd like to
initiate yourself!

A Magic with Tet

Our fear of the unfamiliar can be rooted in ancestral fears of getting hurt. We find that protection spells are often helpful. After setting up the space, if possible, with the usual incense, oil, or candle, take the Tet from your lot bag and hold it between cupped hands. (If you don't have the lots with you, visualize Tet.)

Take deep breaths and set will and intention, which is to know that Tet is there. Know also that it is you who are holding it; it does not hold you because it is enclosed by your cupped hands and cannot get out and take over. Using the lot Tet in this way will activate it as benevolent averting magic.

After reciting the lot poem, say the following words. If you are performing the spell for another person, replace "I" and "me" with the name of that person.

By the Ancestors on whose shoulders I stand

By the Ancestors who hear all and know all and have seen all the worlds

Stand by me so I'll know the right path
Stand by me so I'll walk without fear.

Stand by me so that, if I trip, I won't fall
And if it is needed, then show the path out.
Selah

10

 י

Yod

Future possibility

Yod is for future, or things
you must do

Spirit commanding
Saying "maybe" won't do

Yod indicates the probability that something will take place on occasion, though not often. Like He, it signals the presence of a benevolent power in the action or situation for which the lot casting is consulted.

Yod usually shows up when querents ask about the future. As mentioned, lots do not predict specific future events, but they do point out patterns and where those patterns might lead. In modern Hebrew, unlike classical Hebrew, verbs that refer to the future start with the letter Yod, so that lot is interpreted as describing possible future situations. We are invited to look at those patterns, at their possible outcomes, and, if needed, to change them.

This implies, of course, that the patterns exist or are in the making and that the querent can affect them. More specific information may come from the other letters in the same casting coupled with the energy the seer picks up on.

Because the name Yahweh (or Ya, as is preferred by AMHA) starts with the letter Yod, this lot in a casting sometimes indicates that a godform is involved in the situation being addressed or, more generally, in the querent's life. The message may be from any godform(s) of the AMHA tradition. But since we cast for people of any spiritual tradition, and lot casters can come from any spiritual tradition besides AMHA, the lot may refer to any other power from other spiritual paths—though usually this will indicate power(s) that have commonalities with our own.

The seer will likely be given a sense of which type of power is involved, but this is not always the case and is not usually necessary. Sometimes, it is more than enough to know that spirit, as the person being read for understands it, is present.

The letter Yod may also indicate that a godform will soon get involved. As always, it will be the gift of the seer to have clarity about what it means, aided by the rest of the lots in the cast.

The only power that Yod never represents is the merman god, Dagon, because he has his own lot. Dagon is represented only by the letter Nun and by no other. Why this is the case is unknown, but it is handed-down tradition.

Something to remember is this: If the querent asks how to make a really grave decision, the presence of a godform does not mean that one should follow lot-casting advice blindly. In such a case, we recommend that you always consult with another seer of your tradition, one worthy of trust.

A Meditation with Yod

Many questions can be explored if meditating on Yod. Here is one meditation journey you can take:

You are in the desert, surrounded by rocks that are tan and mauve and rust colored in the bright light. You have been walking a gentle uphill path for a while. Walking is easy, the slope is not steep and the warmth of the day still has the mildness of late spring.

You reach the edge of a plateau where the High Place is, the sacred site you wish to go to. The sky is pale blue but edging toward the cobalt blue it will have all summer, and there are still a few of the fleecy winter clouds left. The air smells dry and hot and dusty, but the sun is not white hot, as it will be later in the year, and the light wind brings the spring scents of wild thyme and mint.

You crest the hill and stand on the flat, rust-colored mesa. Amidst trees, you see the top of a small, mud-brick temple just ahead; the grove and the High Place are enclosed by a low mud-brick wall. Just ahead of you, a half-open wicker gate hangs from leather hinges. You walk forward, push it open, and step into the sacred area within.

Immediately, you feel a heightened sense of peace. There are trees all around a shady grove, with wide, green crowns and powerful trunks rooted in the red-brown dust. A low, sturdy altar stands there, carved roughly from red-veined rock. A small circle of stone benches and chairs surround it, allowing one to sit facing it.

There are two stelae set on pedestals beyond the altar, and you can see flower donations on them and you smell incense donations smoldering in finely carved stone bowls. The air is scented with a mixture of incense and the wild aromatic plants growing all around.

You feel a deep peace. You close your eyes and let your soul reach out. Now you can touch the sacred that is there . . . and ask what you have come to ask.

A Magic with Yod

There are many incantations that can be done with each of the lots in a set, and Yod is no exception. Here is one example of how you can use Yod for a magic.

Let's assume you wish to know which godform or power was/is present in an impending situation. You may not, in our tradition, demand that the godform show itself to you. That is their choice and theirs only. But you can ask them politely if they would reveal who they are so that you can better assess what their message means and what lies ahead.

Yod, Yod, who is all the elohim

Who looks at me kindly?
Which Power are you?

What is your Name
and what gift does it bring?

Yod, Yod, please open my eyes
Yod, Yod, please open my heart.
Yod give me the insight
that I have come to seek.
Selah

11

כ

Kaf

Cupped hand

Kaf is the palm that holds
Blessings and gifts

Take what is given, let
Rich blessings flow

The lot Kaf is a cupped palm. It tells us that a mystical cupped hand is poised to pour down blessings on us and/or the situation we have asked the lots about, and that the gifts will be or already are pouring down on the querent. Due to the hot climate of Israel, the imagery that people associate with Kaf is of a fine, gentle, cooling rain that is falling down. The blessings are already there, whether we have noticed or not. Sometimes, Kaf means that a specific action taken by the querent already has the approval of power(s).

The letter Kaf does not predict dramatic gifts—no winning the lotto or any other spectacular blessing of the type that could flip-flop a person's life. The gifts from Kaf, the blessing hand, are gentle, although they can be substantial. To receive them, one needs to do exactly nothing.

People tell us that they can find it hard to accept that blessings are just there. They think they should have "done something" to deserve them. But Kaf simply blesses us for *being*, not for *doing*. One does not have to "deserve" Kaf.

As for those of us who practice AMHA, we know that we can just stand there and let the blessings pour down. No other action is required; these blessing already exist and are already happening. It does help to be aware of their presence, though, since they affect our current situation, and being aware of Kaf's gifts may, for example, help us feel more confident about something. So the letter Kaf in a lot casting gives us a useful heads-up.

The presence of Kaf in the casting always implies, without saying so directly, that we are not to prevent ourselves from receiving. Other lots in the casting may clarify and make Kaf's message more specific. People have come to us sometimes and said that they had gotten Kaf in a lot casting, "but nothing has happened yet." We usually point out that the gentleness of Kaf's blessing may not be obvious, or that it may become more evident later. Noticing it and feeling the effects may take time, which is why finding Kaf in a casting is such a help. Sometimes, looking back after the fact, one sees that Kaf's gifts were, in fact, happening. They were there, whether we noticed or not.

A Meditation with Kaf

Because of the inordinately difficult time people have simply accepting gifts from power(s), it is sometimes needed to meditate on Kaf each day for a week. The meditation will work better if one physically holds the lot between one's palms or lays it over one's heart.

As always set the space, use the oil or light or incense, and set will and intention specific to what you wish to achieve.

> You are walking in the woods, and the air is comfortably warm. A gentle drizzle of rain is falling pleasantly on you, just barely perceptible, totally comfortable, and you find it agreeably cooling. And as you walk, you know that this gentle rain is blessings, gifts to you from the benevolent power(s) presiding over your life, spirit (as you understand it) and/or ancestors.

You do not need to know from whom it comes for you to ben-
efit, and you do not need to have done anything to get them; the
mystical cupped palm raining down gifts on you is just there,
tilted, gently pouring. All you need to do to receive joy from it
is to become aware of it, to acknowledge that the blessing gifts
are for you. They have always been there, ready for you to notice
them. Allow yourself to accept them, for such gifts are not about
something you do, but about who you are.

A Magic with Kaf

We like to say that Kaf spells are "spells of encouragement." Ado-
lescents, especially, who often are struggling to know their own
worth, can find this spell, if chanted daily, of great help.

So can adults. Besides chanting Kaf as an encouragement
spell, if a person is also willing to do other work that comple-
ments Kaf's power—such as a daily practice with Kaf meditation
to help encouragement—then regardless of age, this incantation works equally well. It can deepen the understanding—and
acceptance—that blessings are present.

After reciting the lot poem for Kaf go on to say:

Kaf gifting hand
Gentle rain on parched soil

Cool like the shade
under the sacred Tree
Showering your blessing upon me

Help me to know you are there
Help me know what you are
Selah

12

ל

Lamed

Learned person or to learn

Lamed is learning or one
Who does so

Points to the places
Your learning must go

The word *lamed* in Hebrew is related to the verb "learning." The lot Lamed is sometimes there to encourage one to pursue further learning. A frequent example would be a querent who is not sure whether they should quit school or continue with their studies or their professional or technical training. The querent usually identifies what area of additional learning or training is being pointed to.

So Lamed can be there to point the querent to learn, perhaps by studying something new or by becoming more accomplished at something they may already be doing. But Lamed can also be saying that before acting, the person needs to get more information about a situation in their life. So Lamed can show up when a querent wonders if they should accept a new job, get that new apartment, or become serious with a recent romantic interest or break up instead. It has shown up when somebody was dithering whether to buy something that is a major expense.

What Lamed says, in all such cases, is, "You need to know more. Do your homework; find out more before deciding. Discover the practical aspects of this."

Lamed can also be saying that a querent who is not currently teaching might consider teaching or instructing or in some way sharing with others something they know. Or, when people come asking the lots if they should seek a spiritual mentor or teacher and become learners on a spiritual path, Lamed in the cast may confirm that they indeed need to do that. It also says strongly that they must "learn more" about the mentor or teacher before they begin. This means doing some research, finding out whether the person they will be learning from is ethical, knowledgeable, and respectful of their students.

A Meditation with Lamed

You are walking in a clean, quiet city. You have been walking comfortably, lost in thought, pondering what to do about that new lover or about that new job, or about kids or in laws or the people at work. You have some ideas but are not sure which plan to follow, or even if you wish to, in fact, follow any of them.

You find yourself on a quiet street with fine trees all along it. There is a tall, lovely building before you, and over the large oaken door, in a fancy script, is written "Library." You feel drawn to the building. It promises answers.

You go inside. It is welcoming; there are books on tall shelves, and wide, comfortable stepping stools make them easy to reach. There are unobtrusive people ready to help you find answers if you chose to ask them for assistance. You walk along the shelves and look for the books that have the answers you need—books on self-healing or growth, books on how to make the best decision, books about workplaces and work life, books about life and relationships.

You pick several and take them to a table with a comfortable chair where you start to read. Take your time. As you gather information, discover what other questions must be asked. Read calmly, without pressure; in this magical library, you have time to find the answers you need.

You sense powers around you, there to favor your learning, favor your finding the answers to your questions. Slowly, as you leaf through the volumes, new questions come to you. Are there details that you have not looked at enough? What minor things that really aren't minor do you need to learn more about? Are there legal issues, and do you need to find people who are qualified to help?

You may need to come back to this Otherworld library to learn what you need a little bit at a time. That is good. It will give you more time to learn well.

A Magic with Lamed

After preparing your space, recite the lot poem for Lamed, then continue with:

By Lamed the lot that says I need knowledge

By Lamed the lot that invites me to learn
By Lamed the lot that will sharpen awareness
Great Powers let Lamed throw light on my path.
Selah

This incantation especially helps people who are afraid to learn more about something important in their life. Kaf can aid them in overcoming that fear.

13

מ

Mem

Water, depth

Mem is like mayim
Its waters are Deep

Under its waves there are
Secrets to keep

Mem is related to מים (*mayim*), the Hebrew word for "water." Mem in lot casting represents the depths in each of us, the ocean of our soul. Mem says that we need to meditate to achieve awareness, an awareness and insight deeper than the one we currently have now. Normally, it refers to a specific situation, but it can also refer to how it counsels us to lead our life in general. This would then mean that we need to live a "deeper" life, to look below the surface of things, to know how to go deep into ourselves where we can better understand.

This reading of Mem applies even if we have already thought extensively or even meditated on the topic we are asking the lots about. Some people prefer not to look at some things too closely, but Mem challenges us to have the courage to dive deep into the sea of our soul and thus learn and grow and heal.

If the querent is already on a spiritual path, Mem suggests more meditation for deeper knowledge. Other times, though, Mem suggests that we need to start such a practice of deep meditation or resume the one we have neglected. For the more experienced in such work, it means "go deeper still." For the neophyte, it means learn how to go past simple "relaxation" and pretty visions of rainbows and unicorns and develop a practice that includes how to go into greater depths where our innermost and most momentous truths reside.

Whether experienced practitioner or neophyte, diving into the sea of your soul can require a certain amount of courage. We always recommend seeking help from an experienced, qualified, and ethical practitioner, especially if the issues about which you need to delve deeper have anything at all to do with trauma.

On occasion, if Mem appears with Bet, it is asking us to use deep meditation to tighten the relationship to our "house"; that is, to learn to relate more closely to the soul energy of our ancestry or spiritual lineage. This has sometimes been humorously referred to as that gentle ancestor's reproach: "You never write, you never call."

Mem does not ask us to blindly throw ourselves into tempestuous waters, even if the issue we are to meditate on more deeply is difficult. We should instead go deep enough, past the turmoil and roiling, that we find the places within that are quiet and still and where answers or healing lie. Mem, like an ocean, has a surface that may be all roiling tempest; with practice, however, one is sure to get to the quiet below. Perhaps not immediately, but over time, Mem leads us to that deep place of peace, where people often tell us that they had their first encounter with the wise one(s) who know(s).

A Meditation with Mem

You are on a beach, and the blue-green ocean ahead is large and welcoming and beautiful. You may never have gone swimming, but now you are not afraid to go in; you know you have gills and can breathe underwater.

The water feels good on your skin, and a gentle current carries you out. It will bring you back any time you wish. Now you are far from the shore. All you hear is the breath of the sea; all you feel is the pleasure of warm sun on your skin and pleasant cool water. You start to dive down, easily breathing in the water, so easily that you barely notice transitioning to using your gills. You dive into the depths of the blue.

There is beautiful life underneath—small, colorful fish swimming around; coral and seahorses; large, lazy fish; bright red starfish; and stately mantas like aquatic angels, flying slowly above you and past as you go deeper and deeper into the inky blue.

There, just below you, smiling up at you and bidding you welcome, awaiting you patiently on a large, flat rock, sits the "wise one who knows." You ask your questions, then return to the surface from the deep and swim home.

The wise one is always there to answer your questions. You can come back again and again.

A Magic with Mem

Set the space, recite the lot poem for Mem, then continue with:

*By the power of breast and
by the power of womb*

*By the power of the Heavens
and the Abyss below*

*Help me dare ask my questions
in the Sea of my Soul*

*let me delve in the depths
and find answers within
Selah*

14

נ

Nun

Dagon, the merman

Nun is the Merman, who
Gifts from the sea

Land gifts he brings too,
Both barley and fish

Nun symbolizes the god Dagon, a merman. He is an ancient deity who probably originated in Mesopotamian mythology about 3000 BCE or earlier. Mesopotamia was, along with Egypt, a superpower, so their cultural influence spread far and wide, reaching westwards even to ancient Israel. So Dagon is one of the few gods who, though born among Sumerians and Akkadians and whose pantheon otherwise differs greatly from ours, ended up also in the Hebrew/Canaanite belief systems. He probably was originally the god of early fishermen and coastal farmers, since he is sometimes depicted as a merman who carries a gift of fish in one hand and barley in the other; that is, he is bringer of balanced gifts from both land and sea.

He is depicted as a virile and muscled god with a proud bearded face and a fish tail that begins at the belly button and takes the place of legs. Dagon in a casting brings balanced gifts, which can mean an impending increase in income, joy for some positive event in one's life, or the resolution of an ongoing issue. Dagon never brings dramatic or spectacular gifts, like winning the lotto, that can upset the balance in one's life. His gifts are always in balance—gifting both body and soul, for example.

In our experience, Dagon frequently shows up and offers his balanced gift expressly to someone who has a habit of expecting scarcity in their life. The merman god's appearance in a lot casting may point to a current imbalance that his gift will rectify. But for balance to be regained, one must accept Dagon's gift.

Unlike the gentle gifts of Kaf (the cupped hands) which, as was discussed previously, require no action at all on our part, the merman god is a bit more demanding. He requires us to be proactive, to move to get his gifts. Therefore, depending on the other lots in the casting, the casting of Nun may also be a warning: If we always insist on waiting to be given blessings, sadly hoping that they will materialize somehow instead of actively reaching for them, or if we are afraid of change so do not make the necessary moves to get our gifts, then we will maintain the imbalance in our life; the merman will swim away, and his offer of gifts will be withdrawn.

A Meditation with Nun

You are standing on the seashore on a fine sunny day, reflecting on the lack in your life, wondering how to achieve a result you really wish for.

Hearing a change in the sound of the waves, you look up. There, farther out on the waters, you see magic. It is Dagon, the merman. He is a powerful godform—broad shouldered, small waisted, his curly black hair gleaming in the sun. He gives you a friendly nod when he sees you looking and starts swimming toward you. As he swims closer, he rises higher from the water. When he is close to the shore, you notice that there is fish in one hand and barley in the other, and he is holding them out to you.

You frown, wondering what that is about. He gestures invitingly, and you begin to understand. These are gifts that he has come here to give you. Gifts that are balanced, gifts of the land and the sea. You hesitate. He nods—yes, they really are for you, if you will have them.

But he does not come closer. Why is that?

He gestures again. He wants you to move a few steps forward, to come partway into the water to take the gifts from his hand. You wonder why. Perhaps you get a bit annoyed. Surely, he can bring them.

Then you realize that Dagon is not testing you; he simply cannot come closer to shore; his large fish tail does not allow him to swim in shallow waters. It is the way of things. It really is you who must move. So now you understand that it is up to you. You must roll up your trousers or skirt, then wade into the water if you want to get what you need. You don't need to go far, knee-high deep at most. But only when you are near and able to hold out your hands, only by indicating willingness to come to him to accept his gifts, can you actually get them from him.

Somehow you understand that even this may not be enough. You need to speak up. You need to ask for the gifts. All the while that you are thinking, he is smiling at you, patiently waiting but inviting you to move. Even beckoning.

Now his friendly smile also tells you that if you don't move and if you don't ask, he will have to swim away, taking his gifts with him, and you will be left on the shore. Left with nothing.

So you step into the shallow water and take careful steps. When you are close enough, you reach for the fish and the barley and say, "I would like to have my gifts now." Then he holds them

*out to you. You take his gifts in your hands. With a nod and a
smile, he turns and swims away.*

*With those balanced gifts that you have claimed, that are
now yours and can bring you blessings, you can return to your
day and your life.*

A Magic with Nun

After reciting lot poem for Nun, set intention and will on the
goal you wish to achieve, then say this incantation:

*Dagon Merman, bring me your gifts
please come, swim close*

See, I step forward and forward again . . .

*Dagon Merman, as I step forward
make these waters be shallow
and warm*

*Dagon, may your gifts rest on me lightly.
Selah*

15
ס
Samekh

Bliss, usually in the meaning of great spiritual fulfillment
or even shamanistic ecstasy

Samekh is bliss of the
Heart and the Soul
And of the body
and never is small

Samekh is related to the Hebrew word *sameakh*, שׂמח, meaning "happy" or "merry." But unlike in modern Hebrew usage, Samekh does not refer to good feelings like cheerfulness or any of the less intense emotions connected to feeling good. In lot casting, Samekh is about very powerful, intense feelings, like a deep sense of spiritual peace or fulfillment or even of ecstatic bliss.

Samekh at its mildest refers to the joy a parent might have when holding their child, both deep and immense; or to seeing a truly loved one again after a very long time. It is experienced when greeting somebody cherished as they return from war.

At its most powerful, Samekh can refer to the ecstasy of touching powers in meditation. Mystics of all types, from shamans to modern-day practitioners, have described connecting to the sacred and reaching a state of ecstasy as a joy so intense that it borders on pain. Some think of it as the peak moment of many a spiritual practice.

Other traditions maintain that this ecstatic state can be reached only if following a specific religious or spiritual path. We do not agree with this last view. Spiritual paths from all over the world and from many different timelines know the ecstatic feelings Samekh represents. All kinds of powers have made themselves known, since the most ancient societies, and have touched humans who sought that contact.

As discussed earlier, among the Hebrews, these powers ranged from "high" (we prefer to say "senior") goddesses and gods to the "smaller" ("junior") bnei elohim in their various forms, such as angels, ancestors, nature spirits, and any other godforms that were and still are thought to be reachable through the ecstatic experience(s). People who could attain ecstasy could do so whether they were reaching for gods of the city or of the tribe—which were their community gods—or godforms to which they might devote their private reverential practice.

Literature on tribal shamanic initiations are filled with examples of mystical encounters with the numinous. Rather than pigeonholing that bliss as possible only in one specific set of beliefs, we think that any path can lead to it. To us, it is important that ultimately the practitioner's experience will be intensely their own, transcending paths and traditions, barely describable, just as the numinous in whatever form is ultimately barely describable. Samekh, being sensation not thought, is hard to express in words.

We have found that, regardless of what godform(s) we are devotees of (or none), Samekh in a lot casting points to spiritual experiences ranging from the great fulfillment of finding the right spiritual path—described by some as a sense of coming home at last—to the full-powered ecstatic bliss of being in the presence of a godform.

Today, seers of many traditions are often asked by querent to tell them which spiritual path to take. Or they ask if they have made the right choice. Or if they are doing the right things on the path that they are already on. Or which godform(s) to follow.

Samekh will not suggest a godform or power, but if the querent is already on a path, the lot may confirm to them that they have already reached a spiritual home, or that they may be able to, which offers a sense of finally having a place to belong—a calming and intense experience at the same time.

Sometimes Samekh says that an ecstatic experience of enlightenment is on our horizon if we seriously continue following the spiritual practices or exercises of whatever path we have chosen. Samekh, not being predictive, does not guarantee this will happen, but says instead that the current direction makes it likely.

A Meditation with Samekh

We find that meditation with Samekh is simple but not easy. This is true if you are a seeker—a person who is looking for a spiritual home by taking a path that will feel truly yours—or if, outside any specified formal path, you are simply seeking the bliss of direct connection to your power(s).

Hold the lot Samekh in your hand. Anoint yourself. Chant the lot poem until you feel yourself sinking deep into a meditation state. When you feel that you are deep enough, open your inner eyes and look around you.

> You find that you are walking on a path. You are back in the landscape that you know so well, and it feels good to know that you have been here before. You are comfortable and peaceful, but you are still unsure where this path will lead, still seeking answers.
>
> You see another path ahead, one that branches from the one that you are on; it is not a path you have followed before. As you

approach it, you recognize it. Though you have not been on it, you know: This path leads to the Otherworld, to the home of your spirit where you can feel further your connection with power(s). It is a journey for your soul that you may have had fears about. You step off the path you are on and take the branching one.

Somehow, you now know that it will be easy to stray from this path, to get distracted, so remind yourself of your intention: You have set out to at last find your spiritual home and even to meet the power(s) that await(s) to embrace you and accept you as their devotee.

You keep walking. Observe what is around you as you go. There may be tree spirits pointing your way by waving their branches; four-legged furry ones or two-legged feathered ones— all the little children of the Mother—may be there to be helpful and show you your way. There may be a guardian—tall, strong, and kind—standing at a crossroads. You can stop to ask directions, and, smiling at you, the guardian tells you where need to go next.

The description is interrupted here because Samekh meditation is in many ways unique. The goal is frequently to identify one's path. This can usually be achieved with a regular practice of meditation with other suitable lots, together with Samekh, depending on the circumstances. Consult an experienced seer if you need clarification.

A more momentous application of Samekh meditation is to use it to learn how to connect to a specific godform. Such a goal appears simple, but simple does not mean easy. Think of Samekh meditation as one that has as its goal an ongoing practice rather than a single event. Attempting to touch power(s) for the first time in one long sitting requires effort and often leads to an exhausting meditation with little or no result, which makes it hard to do consistently. It's better to do it gradually. Most people report that successfully connecting directly to power requires a practice of consistent, short meditations over time instead of a one-time meditation marathon.

As this is a task best undertaken in small steps, it yields better results if planned—rather like the long-range journey discussed in chapter 9, but without the risks of traumatic encounters, because its aim is only to connect you to power. When wishing to reach states of ecstasy, it may be helpful to think of the meditation as a hike through the wilderness that may require days or even weeks to reach one's goal; therefore, it must be done in stages with breaks in between.

Just as with a deep wilderness trek in the physical world, it is important to go only as far each time on the Otherworld path as to easily be able to go back to base camp (i.e., ordinary consciousness). This is so you can rest up and ponder on what you have experienced so far; you will learn something each time. Each stage has value. Each stage brings you closer. We recommend not being impatient. Unlike a hike in ordinary reality, in this one you will not lose the progress you have made once you return to base camp. You can resume the Samekh trek another day.

However, what you must do every time before leaving the Otherworld landscape to return to ordinary reality is to firmly set the intention to pick up the Samekh journey where you left off so that your progress will resume when you next return. So it bears repeating: do not exhaust yourself attempting to get there in one meditation session. A journey to find one's spiritual home, or even to connect with the numinous, is a truly big deal.

A Samekh Working with the purpose of "touching" power(s) requires patience. Some of our members have practiced this for as long as a year, going back to the same journey again and again—always learning something, always growing stronger, always starting where they left off—until they reached their goal. The practice to find one's path or one's godform can be arduous and requires patience. Practice with perseverance, and you will find your path leading your spiritual home. Ultimately, the best suggestion we can make is to persist.

Here is an important reminder: When working with Samekh, especially, being critical and judgmental of your meditation is a sure way to delay achieving the intended goal. A frequent mistake, occurring particularly with beginners using Samekh, is to ask, "Am I there yet?" Or "When will I get there?" Or, most often, "Am I doing this wrong?" Do no doubt yourself. Simply come back after resting, bring awareness back to the meditative state, and keep going.

A Magic with Samekh

By Samekh, great Powers,
great Ashera and El

By Samekh great Powers
great Ancestors all
Be friend(s) to my soul
Bring Samekh to me

and show me the path
to achieve holy bliss

16

ע

Ayin

Well, source, seer's eye

---

*Ayin means well, and the
Deep Seeing Eye*

*Seek Seer's wisdom, seek
Knowledge from High.*

Ayin in Hebrew means "source of water"; it also means a "water well." In arid regions, wells were crucial to survival. Being recognized as a source of life, often a well was associated with a sacred grove or High Place. In some cultures around the world, even to this day, people seek insight by gazing at water in a well, a form of divination called scrying.

Ayin in lot casting means both "seeing eye" (the eye of the seer) and "well where (mystical) knowledge can be found." At its simplest, Ayin means consult a seer or meditate for answers.

The seer's knowledge was seen as a gift from the elohim (powers). And among the elohim, stars were included. Seeking their answers required a state of meditation for which the metaphor was a descent to the wells of wisdom, since at night, before telescopes, one could best see stars from inside a well.

In a modern lot casting, we think of Ayin as a suggestion to seek through meditation the metaphysical answers to a specific issue or question. So when Ayin shows up in a lot casting, it asks us to go down into the well of wisdom to find an answer, or to "drink in" information of a spiritual nature. For many seers in our tradition, the well is a liminal place; that is, one of the places where human and spiritual spheres meet and overlap and where, therefore, one can find answers.

We have been asked: If Ayin shows up in a casting, can it ever suggest that we (the querent[s]) have a dry well? It never means this. It merely invites use to make use of Ayin the well or eye.

If Ayin is in a lot casting with a beginner, it is telling them to practice, to "go to the well" more frequently, which, in this case and depending on the other lots, may simply mean that they need to start learning meditation. Many neophytes find Ayin encouraging, therefore, since they often wonder if they can hope to reach higher/deeper knowing in the first place.

Ayin sometimes also means "consult a seer," especially if it shows up when we are casting for ourselves. Or if the question is in some way a weighty one, Ayin means "go seek a second opinion." As a reminder, in lot casting the answers are suggestions rather than commands, and a second opinion is recommended to help clarify the message.

A Meditation with Ayin

If you have the sight, the seer's eye, this is a meditation that can help hone it.

> *You are walking on a wide path, and sunset is near. You can see the land around you is filled with flowers. Their perfume reaches you. A wafting wind is gentle on your skin. You feel quiet joy and deepening peace at each step that you take.*

You come around a curve in the landscape, and you can smell the scent of pure water. The well you are seeking is close. It is perhaps unlike any well you have seen before. It is surrounded by a tall wall of red stones. For a moment, you may wonder how one can get to the water when the walls around it are so high, but as you approach, you notice there is an opening in the red wall. As you get closer, you see stairs leading down. Far below is the glint of clean water.

This is an ancient place, and this is how the ancients built wells in this arid land. The tall walls provide shelter from the sun, and broad winding stairs lead one down to the water that lies in cool shade deep at the bottom.

The stairs ahead of you are dry and wide and easy, so you begin to descend. There are comfortable handrails carved into the rock, and as you go down, farther down, you catch the gleam of the water. There is still enough light to see that there is wide, comfortable ledge at the bottom for people to stand on.

When you step off the stairs onto the ledge, you notice that seats have been carved into the rock. The water sparkles clean and pure, it smells fresh and cool. You sit and breathe in the cool, moist air. Feel the deepening peace.

When you look up at last, you see that night has fallen, and stars are studding the dark velvet sky. You can feel your inner eye opening, and you are filled with insight. You fall into a reverie. Drink it in deeply before you return.

A Magic with Ayin

This can be done for yourself or someone else. Change the wording accordingly.

By Ayin the Well where
deep knowledge resides

By Ayin the Seeker's eye,
that sees the high truths

Lend me (them) your power
so I (they) may have clear Sight

Lend me (them) your power
So I (they) know what I (they) See
Selah.

17

פ

Pe

Mouth, speaking your truth

Pe is the mouth and the
Words that it speaks

It means speak out or speak up
Or speak for, or speak deep

The energy of Pe always encourages; it tells us that what we know is worth sharing. Pe always tells us to speak up or speak out, and sometimes to teach what we know. For example, Pe may suggest that our promotion at work will soon have us needing to speak to or instruct others. We have also found Pe showing up for people who excel at something, but it has not occurred to them to share what they know. Pe is a help to the shy person, because it conveys that their voice or their knowledge has value and that they should go ahead and speak up.

Pe may mean that the time is coming to share what we have spiritually achieved or share what our struggles are to help others with, for example, the initial difficulties of trying to start a spiritual practice. Keep in mind, however, that in the culture in which our tradition is rooted, Pe is never an invitation to proselytize, a practice that our belief system does not find acceptable, no matter how well intentioned.

Pe is also an encouragement for clear, firm, effective communication with others—in any area of our life.

Sometimes, Pe flat out tells us to step forward and speak our truth, to speak up and speak out—at home or at work, with acquaintances or friends, or with relatives or romantic relationships. The goal is not to encourage altercation. On the contrary, Pe in a lot casting implies that if we don't have the habit or skills to communicate what is needed, we should learn how to do so. The whole point of Pe is for our voice to be heard, which will not happen if we do not know how this is done. (Learning to improve our communication skills is something to consider, especially if we are lot casting.)

Uncomfortably, yet often, Pe says that we need to stand up with integrity and clarity of voice for people or for ideas we value, rather than keep silent. The use of put-down humor or jokes that belittle when objecting to something or correcting a behavior is incompatible with the energy from Pe. That is passive aggression, which demeans the one who does it as well as those who are the victims of it. In our tradition, it is always dishonorable to make somebody else feel small. There are a very few exceptions to that in our belief, such as when somebody is trying to bully us, to make us feel small. We may need to reestablish the power parity by using our communication skills to get them to relinquish their "top dog" attitude.

A Meditation with Pe

We find this type of meditation to be useful in helping find one's voice. We recommend daily practice for those who are shy or who for some reason are anxious about speaking their truth.

You are in a room, and you are surrounded by people who are talking. You may know some of them, or not. You notice that one or more of them are saying something that you do not agree with. As they continue talking, you realize that there is more to it—what they have been saying refers to you, or it may be about other people. Either way, it dawns on you that what they are saying would be an offense to those they are talking about.

They are laughing, while engaging in put downs. You are embarrassed; you don't know what to do. You are afraid that they will say they are only joking and accuse you of being a spoilsport if you object. Should you open your mouth and speak out? Should you not? You are resolved to say something, yet you find that you cannot. You try again, but your voice is gone. Allow yourself to sink deeper and to ponder this.

When you are ready, ask yourself some questions: Is what they are saying actually wrong? Why have you lost your voice to object? How did you lose that power? And when? Did you ever have a voice? You think that you must have, but it is now lost. You need that voice back. Where do you go to find your voice again?

As you ponder these questions, you are going still deeper. The room with the people has vanished, and you have begun walking in a gray landscape, surrounded by grey hills; they are high and too near, and the air feels constricting and close.

You realize that because your voice is lost, you cannot freely breathe. What does your voice even sound like?

Your voice . . . imagine what colors it has, what shape, what it feels like, what it smells like. Keep on walking, then start looking around; see if you find it.

You may find it on this first try, or discover that you need to come back again to this place to learn how. Keep on trying; eventually you will have learned how to find your voice. It's not complicated; all you need to do is to work on taking it back.

With this realization, the grayness around you pales, and you can breathe much better. You can go back to your here and now, gently and slowly, and return to the space where you started this meditation.

Now that you know that you can find your own voice, simply come back as often as needed to find it, strengthen it, and make it clear.

A Magic with Pe

After setting the space and intention and reciting the lot poem for Pe, say:

By the six-winged ones

*By the Seraphim
whose kiss
burn lips like a flame
and opens the mouth
for true speech*

*Seraphim strengthen
my voice*

*Rafael
Gabriel
Uriel
Azriel*

Walk with me
guard me
as I speak my truth.

Walk with me, guard me
as I open my mouth

walk with me, teach me
so I learn to be heard.
Selah

18
צ
Tsadiq

Wisdom

Tsadiq a Wise One in
One heart combines
Knowledge and Kindness
It's what makes one Wise.

A *tsadiq* (צדיק in Hebrew) is a wise person. In the popular view, that means a person who combines intellectual knowledge (i.e., learning) with kindness, which is a quality of the heart and soul. We cannot be wise if we only know stuff, if we only operate from our fact-laden, analytical brains; nor can we be wise if we are operating strictly from our heart. Knowledge without kindness puts us in a cold, lonely world. Kindness without knowledge at best stumbles lovingly in the dark. At worst, it may lead us to hurt others despite our best intentions, because we neglected to get all the information. In such cases, our attempts to help somebody may end badly.

Wisdom has been highly valued since ancient times, not only by the primitive Hebrew tribes but also other cultures in antiquity; and it is still valued to this day. Historically, wisdom would have been one of the attributes of the great God El, father of the ancient gods, who was also called the "good god." We would say as AMHA today that it is this combination of knowing and compassion that made El the most powerful in our ancient pantheon.

In Hellenistic days, wisdom was considered of such value that it eventually was personified and became a goddess, Sophia (which means "wisdom" in Greek). Over time, for the Greeks and Gnostics and later for the kabbalists (as the Shekinah), wisdom became God's feminine face.

As to how this applies to humans, if Tsadiq is in a lot casting, it may mean that we need to combine knowledge with kindness when dealing with ourselves and others and/or that we should connect to the "kind one who knows" within us or seek contact with Father El and/or a power that has the characteristics of combined knowledge and kindness. Tsadiq may also be telling us where we need to direct its energies. People often think that Tsadiq in a lot casting means "be kind to others." It does, but we find that often it is there to remind us to be kind to ourselves. There is a proverb that says that without both, one is merely half kind.

If we forget kindness to ourselves in relationships, we may develop or reinforce painful patterns in which we give without getting, which is acting unwisely. Tsadiq in a casting can even be a strong warning that knowledge and kindness are both missing in some aspect of our relationship.

Wisdom, that combination of knowledge and kindness, is the quality that allows us heal ourselves, if needed, and/or be of benefit to others. Tsadiq may tell us to be mindful of being knowledgeable but also to have warmth. A person who has the qualities of Tsadiq has their strength and their knowledge rooted in compassion. Its appearance in a lot casting may be reminder to keep heart and head in good balance.

A Meditation with Tsadiq

This meditation is intended to help us become more proficient at balancing knowledge and kindness to improve our relationships with self and others.

You are walking over a lovely green meadow toward a small wood not far off. The trees there are in flower, and on the ground you see flowers everywhere. You're really looking forward to reaching the pretty trees and comfortably resting beneath them and listening to singing birds.

As you walk, something shifts, appears to change; the green grass that was soft underfoot and the flowers' aroma when you brushed against them are changing somehow. At first, you can't tell exactly what is happening; gradually, though, everything around you becomes increasingly dry and brown. The soft, green, springy grass has turned into a rough, uncomfortable surface that scratches your bare feet; sharp pebbles have appeared. As you continue walking, they get more and more uncomfortable.

This was not how things were supposed to turn out; this is not what you foresaw when you first took the path with the soft green grass. There was a promise of enjoyment and shelter and peace.

A guide, smiling and caring and strong, appears to you, raises a hand gently, and asks you to stop. The guide points to the dreary, dying landscape ahead and begins asking questions to help you understand what has happened.

Take your time to listen to each question. Take your time to think and find answers.

Did you look at the path carefully to see where it led? When you first stepped on it, was the beautiful green grass truly so soft beneath your feet? When did you first notice that it was changing? What made you notice it?

Did you perhaps continue on the path because you didn't want to acknowledge a change for the worse? Did you try to ignore that this was not the beautiful meadow you had hoped for? Perhaps you read the map incorrectly. Did you seek answers only from knowledge and fail to find them? Or did you seek answers only in your heart and not find them? Do you reproach yourself because neither has served you?

Ponder... breathe deeply... allow yourself to slowly find the answers you need. You sought in your brain but didn't find them; you sought in your heart, but that didn't work either.

Your guide will be here, protecting you as you learn how to blend within yourself more knowledge and compassion for others and self. Blend and balance them—and create the alchemy of Wisdom.

A Magic with Tsadiq

As usual, set space and intention and recite the lot poem for Tsadiq. Adjust the pronouns as needed.

By Tsadiq
By Wisdom
Blue flowers for knowledge
red flowers for love

I make them a garland to
wear on my head

I make them a garland
to warm up my heart

Come Wisdom to my heart
Come Wisdom to my head

By Tsadiq soft power
Come Tsadiq soft power
Both knowing
and kind
Selah

19
ק
Quf

Monkey

Quf is the monkey that's
Trapped in your skull

Jumps back and forth
Round and round, never still

Quf (or qof) means "monkey" in Hebrew. Everyone can understand the energy of Quf. Just think of an upset, chattering monkey trapped in a cage. Quf is about thoughts that bounce back
and forth and round and round within the cage of our skull
when we have a dilemma. If we think of Quf this way, we have a
good idea of what the "monkey mind" means.

It is our restless, worried mind; we may be even in a frantic
state, filled with pressure on self and the anxious need to find
a solution or to find a way out, and to do so fast. When we are
in monkey mind, we make ourselves weary by thinking and
rethinking whether we want this or that solution; then, liking
neither of the two extreme options, we start bouncing off the
walls all over again—and we get nowhere. Self-blame for not
finding the solutions may be added to the mix.

Monkey mind can be a type of fear; as such, it narrows our
horizons. It can give us such tunnel vision that we never notice
that the best solution is not choosing between A and B at all but
that C, or maybe D or F, are suitable options—all of which we

are failing to consider because we are so busy being caged by our frantic thoughts.

That said, it is important to remember that lots may be blunt, but they do not cast blame. Quf does not either. So when Quf shows up in a casting, we should refrain from blaming ourselves—a frequent reaction that only increases our stress.

Like other lots, Quf is simply there to hold up a mirror. It tells us we are human and that monkey mind is part of being human, that we need to pay less attention to the frantic emotion of the moment and more to the fact that a situation requiring solutions exists, and that being stressed by this is not wrong or bad or a character defect. With that awareness, we can honor our tense feelings, which makes stepping out of the monkey-mind cage much easier. After all, Quf strongly implies that having bouts of monkey mind pretty much comes with the territory—at least sometimes in one's life.

Pretending to ourselves that monkey mind is not there and trying to force ourselves to function anyway frequently fails to work. Monkey-mind state, while normal, is painful, so will not benefit us in the long run. Quf is there to tell us that the best way to cope is to *not* waste more energy with self-blame but instead to step back, take a few breaths, calm down, and take our time to reconsider what other options may be available.

Quf does not ever mean, "Make up your mind now!" which is how we often feel in monkey-mind state. There is no inherent virtue in fast decisions when instant solutions spring from monkey mind. Let's slow down instead so we can ponder. If we do, we will be doing ourselves the favor of not compounding the already painfully tense condition.

Quf in a casting does not, of course, tell you what the next problem-solving steps should be. Further insight on this will be provided by the other lots in the casting.

A Meditation with Quf

To resolve whatever problem caused us to have monkey mind in the first place, it is best not to start by working on the specifics of the problem at all. We recommend holding off, at least at first, from embarking on solution-seeking long-range journeys.

Instead, we prefer the use of Quf for a series of deep, calming meditations—jocularly referred to elsewhere in this book as "shamanic tourism"; that is, nonthreatening, agreeable vision seeking. For most people, beginning meditations with Quf in this way prepares them to later use more targeted meditation with Quf to address the problem(s) that caused monkey minds in the first place.

If we go into a trance over Quf issues before we are calmer and ready to explore how to tackle the specifics of our issues, we are apt to scare ourselves, which makes the meditation unproductive.

However, if we are experienced in meditation practices and there is competent support available (that we can easily reach out to), then we can allow the person or mentor of our choice to be our "ground crew" and guide as we start a series of more targeted, solution-seeking journeys. Although this is an option, it is still a good idea to do the calming meditations first.

Either way, it is beneficial to seek the comfort and safety of ancestors or guides if they have helped reassure us in the past and if it has calmed monkey mind previously.

You are in a semi-dark room. It has no windows but several heavy glass doors that you believe to be locked. You know that night is falling and that there is an unfriendly rocky landscape outside. You don't like being there. You know you need to leave this room; it feels close somehow, makes you feel caged. It is chillier than you'd like and growing colder. There is nobody else around but there are butterflies in your stomach; you sense a threat, but you know not from what.

There is just enough light in the room to see all the doors ahead of you. You know that each of them leads to a different path, and each could help you get away from the room, but which is the right one? Which one will be safe? You go to one door . . . but what if it's wrong? So you go to another one, but that could be wrong, too. Which door should you take? And that next one, could that be the right one, perhaps? There's nobody you can ask.

You hear the wind rising, and it is getting even colder. The wind rises further and louder and it is getting darker outside; you have trouble even seeing the doors and where the paths outside might lead. You pull your cloak closer against the cold, and you think how nice it would be to be somewhere safe, warm and cozy by a fire with good choices already made.

As you pull the cloak tighter, you feel a necklace. It was not there before. There is a pendant. You touch it; it is ice cold. You raise it to look at it. In the dim light you see it's a beautiful jewel, and Quf is engraved on it. Even though you feel very threatened right now, the pendant feels so reassuring, despite being cold, and it tells you to make yourself breathe slowly, slowly, so you do. As you go deeper, the room begins to feel warmer, and the pendant, too, is warm and comfortably nestling in your in your hand. You look at it again and see that Quf is glowing; you are feeling calmer.

You realize that something has changed. Now you know that this jewel is a talisman, it's a bringer of good. As you realize this, the friendly warmth from it spreads all through your body, and you feel calmer still. In the wind outside, there are comforting voices—your guardians soothing you, calming you. The talisman is telling you that it is okay to have doubts about possible choices; there are answers, and they will come to you. It is the mothers talking, it is the fathers talking, the kind ones, the loved ones who, whether or not you know who they are, have the wise answers.

And as the talisman shines with a brightening, warmer light, you feel even calmer, you begin to believe. Yes, you can find good answers, solutions; though it may take a little time, you begin to believe that you can, and, as you do, the light grows in the room. It gets brighter and brighter until all corners are warmly lit. You see now . . . there is another glass door. One you overlooked before. In fact, there are two . . . and more—more doors and more choices than you saw at first.

As your ancestors' wisdom whispers gently, you will soon know which of the doors you want to take. They are unlocked. And well-lit paths await you beyond. And your choice is not final . . . few choices are . . .

A Magic with Quf

Monkey mind, monkey mind
caught in the cage
What is right, what is wrong?
Going up?
Going down?
Going right?

Going left?

Monkey mind, monkey mind
how will I know?
Go to the Mothers kind
Go to the Fathers kind

seek their embrace

Go to the Ancestors
And ask them for answers

Go to the Ancestors
And ask them for peace.

Monkey mind, monkey mind
Monkey mind hush . . .
Be quiet now and sleep . . .
Selah

20

ר

Resh

The start of a new process, a trailhead

Resh is the head or
Beginnings of things

Also means first, or go
Learn how to think.

The Hebrew letter Resh sounds a lot like the Hebrew word *rosh* (ראש), meaning "head." In a lot casting, Resh alerts us that we are at the beginning of a new process in our life. For those of you who hike, think of this like a trailhead, the start of a path you are about to take.

Rosh does not refer to an event but to the beginning of any process that is potentially ahead that will form a new pattern in your life: a new job may be on the horizon, or you may be on the verge of changing how you manage an existing relationship. It can also indicate that ahead of you is the option, say, of breaking off a relationship.

Other lots in the same cast may suggest that you should or should not engage on a path that lies ahead of you; it is certainly not an invitation to plunge ahead just because Resh is there. Resh simply points our attention to a beginning pattern. Resh never predicts a specific event unless that event is, in itself, the start of a new pattern.

Resh is helpful because it tells us to notice that new elements are present that are birthing new situations. Unless the other lots in the casting say otherwise, Resh does not say whether the potential new process is something good or bad. Like most lots, Resh is neutral and just holding up a mirror or hinting in a direction without judgment of any kind.

A Meditation on Resh

You are walking on a wide path in your favorite city park, amidst beautiful trees that have been carefully planted. There are flowers and bushes—all orderly and tended. You are comfortable ambling along on this well-known path, and you know where it leads. It feels so familiar to be here, because you are here often; you know the trails, you recognize trees you have seen in all seasons—red-golden in fall, silver-white during winter, and budding with green in the spring. It is summer now, and everything is blooming, everything in leaf.

As you walk, you notice ahead of you a wooden sign on a shoulder-high pole. You have not seen it before; it surprises you a little, so you stop to see what the sign says. On the freshly cut wood, you see a large, red Hebrew letter ר*. "Resh," you say aloud. The sign points ahead to a space between trees, to a trailhead you have not noticed before. You peer through the foliage, but from where you stand, it is obscured somewhat by heavier growth. You can see that the path meanders, but you cannot see very far along.*

However, you can tell that the plantings on that trail are not quite the same as what you are used to seeing when you walk in this park. You realize that it must it lead somewhere new; you are not sure where, but you can guess if you ponder. Isn't there a lake somewhere here? Is there not a campground beyond?

You do not know exactly. But you do know that if you step up to this trailhead, it will put you on a path to places in this well-known park that you have yet to explore.

This is not frightening at all. You see now that a new options are there, new walks to take. Now that you know that this path is open, you can choose whether to take it and engage in something different and new or stay on the old, familiar path.

A Magic with Resh

Resh, Resh
a trailhead that's new
Ancestors, ancestors
a new path I see

I can start a new way
I can start on this path

Width differs
length differs
Goals differ, too

Ancestors, ancestors
is this Resh for me?
Ancestors, ancestors
should I go forward?

Ancestors, ancestors
or should I stay?
Selah

21

ש

Shin

Tooth, fang, fire

Shin is the tooth and your
Fangs sharp and white
It is your soul's fire,

Hot flames
Burning bright.

The word Shin (שׁין) in Hebrew means "tooth" or "fang." It assumes that you possess sharp, white, healthy fangs. Their purpose is not to hurt, to rend, to attack, or to kill, so Shin in a casting is not saying that it is time to get violent or go on a bout of rape and pillage; it does remind you, instead, that you do have the ability to use sharp teeth if necessary; that is, to meet difficult situations.

Also, because of its shape, which is reminiscent of flames, Shin refers to that inner flame of vitality or courage or creativity that is deep within us. When Shin shows up in a casting, it may be inviting us to notice we already have that flame within us, that we are perfectly able to reach into ourselves to draw on that life energy.

Shin is the only letter of the lot set that has two separate images to elucidate it, the flame and the fang. The message that either imagery offers is similar: Know that you can reach for the fire in your belly, the source of your inner strength and vitality;

know that you have fangs; know that you can gird your loins, if you choose, and therefore meet challenges.

But Shin goes a step beyond telling us what there is within us; it also tells us that we are, or may soon be, in a situation requiring us to sharpen those fangs; that is, to take some initiative, or speak up, or even be ready to stand our ground, and that we should not be alarmed, since we already come well equipped with the necessary tools. (Besides, sometimes all that is needed is to show we have teeth.)

Above all, Shin says that it is time to reach for that life energy, for that "fire in the belly" that fuels our capacity for action, creativity, and passion.

We have heard people say that they do not have it. But however damped our energy, however long we may not have known of it or refrained from tapping into it, Shin states that now is a good time to find the initiative, or even the courage, to reach for it, even if we have forgotten that we can or have never learned how.

Occasionally, Shin may also mean, "Show your emotions. Be fully authentic. Act with clear conviction and be assertive." We have learned that this message from Shin for showing inner power can confuse or even intimidate some Westerners, whose culture often prefers denying emotions and their expression.

But speaking one's truth or acting decisively does not mean abusing others. Accessing one's inner ability to be creative or powerful or passionate can manifest as very peaceful behaviors. That, too, is a message in Shin.

A Meditation with Shin

You are sitting very comfortably in a small, cozy room with a book in your lap, a blanket keeping you warm. Outside it is raining and perhaps even cold. There are things that need doing outside, but in here is the merry crackling of flames. You turn your head to look at the fire burning brightly in the hearth and notice the fine smell of pine in the room.

Then you think of all that must be done: Perhaps there are people you need to talk to or duties that you need to fulfill or tasks that have not been completed. You tell yourself that you are fine as you are, where you are, but you do not really believe that. There is a lassitude that won't let you get up and go. You know that you have to, and you feel uneasy; things out there don't attend to themselves. But you really don't want to get going; you turn your back to the window so that you can no longer see what awaits outside—that outside with its tasks not yet done. You just stare at your fire as you have done so often before.

As you look at the small leaping flames, you see them slowly growing; you feel more of their warmth. The gentle warmth reaches out to you and, like a hug, wraps around you. The face of your guardian appears in the fire; the flames are its hair and its eyes and its face. The guardian speaks gently to you through the crackling of the fire and says:

"You have been telling yourself that you are fine where you are for a while now, but in truth you are not comfortable, for you know that what needs to be done—what you need to get done—is not happening. Come, get your warmth from me; reach for my heat; let it kindle your own flame within; feel the warmth. It is growing and with it your strength. Reach for it, more and more, and when you are ready, go get done what still needs to be done."

A Magic with Shin

This is an incantation that feels most effective when (after setting space, will, and intention and reciting the lot poem) we chant it while walking three circles. If doing this Working outdoors, a small fire is helpful for focusing. If indoors, a candle or, to be safest, a battery candle light can be used while performing this incantation.

If the Working is on behalf of another, have them walk a circle at the same time as you but in the opposite direction while reciting the incantation with you (or in a call and response if they do not know the words). The motion of going sunrise (clockwise) and moonrise (anticlockwise) strongly grounds this magic and connects it metaphysically to the deep flames within Mother Earth.

Shin, Shin, show
Me your flames

Help me to reach them
and lend me their heat

Shin, Shin, show me my fangs
give me their sharpness
for food or for fight
Selah

22

ת

Tav

Stop, end, bring to a close

Tav is the seal that is set
When all's closed

It stops inaction and
Action alike.

Tav is the last letter of the Aleph-Bet. Therefore, in a lot casting, it signifies "to seal" or "to end." In ancient times, a wax seal was intended to indicate that the content of a letter was final, and once the seal was applied, the content could not be changed, so seals were also affixed to prevent changing the existing content.

So Tav tells us that something in our life needs to end, to be brought to a close, to be "sealed." And that it is up to us to bring that about. Think of stamping down on the wax used for sealing a letter shut. Tav is perhaps the only statement from lots that is close to a command. It tells us, "Stop now."

Tav invites us to act decisively and, if at all possible, with minimal delay. When Tav shows up, it's energy is close to that of an order; so as lot casters, we need to explain its meaning to the querent gently and respectfully, while at the same time not diluting the message.

In our experience, Tav most often refers to situations or patterns that harm us in some way and that need to be discontinued. Often it means that we should stop acting as though we were people of little worth who deserve whatever painful pattern there is in our present life.

If it refers to things like a habit that is harmful or to a toxic relationship, Tav tells us to put a stop to this and/or to get out. Getting out of tricky situations is sometimes like trying to get off a tiger one is riding, but we have learned that Tav never shows up if the situation cannot in any way be changed. For, in fact, even when we think it is so, very few situations in life cannot be changed, and they usually are those involving life-and-limb issues.

Given its energy, we find that Tav can raise delicate issues. Let's say that the situation has a potential for violence, such as a violent partner. The querent wants to leave, but statistics show us that there is more risk, in many cases, when the abused tries to leave. Now Tav has shown up in the reading. Because its meaning is so blunt, and the message to "stop" is unmistakable, the lot caster now finds themselves in a dilemma.

On one hand, the caster must speak clearly that Tav requires the querent to stop being victimized. On the other hand, the ethics when lot casting require us to alert the querent to risks. In such a case, it is best to refer a victim of abuse to specialists who can walk them through the safe steps to take. This is what ethics require. Simply telling them to get out when we know it is potentially dangerous is unethical. So Tav in a lot casting can turn out to give both querent and lot caster a tricky job.

Sometimes, in our experience, Tav may also mean, "Something has ended, stop trying." This is usually the case when a person is struggling with the awareness of or the acceptance of some process or relationship in their life that may be in its death throes, such as a job or a relationship, and they do not wish to see it end. Tav, however, is not a predictor of actual or impending physical death.

A Meditation with Tav

You are looking at some stairs leading down. You know that below is a place for reflection, a place where decisions can be made, so you start going downstairs. You take a calming breath at each step, and go deeper and deeper; feel your breathing get slow and even, until at last you have reached the bottom of the stairs, which have led to a large, comfortable room.

There is your desk, large and beautiful, and your comfortable upholstered chair by it. On the desk, items are scattered about: an ink bottle, an old-fashioned feather pen, and loose papers. You approach and draw the chair back; you sit down and adjust the chair so that you can comfortably write. You notice that the papers are not just any papers, they are important ones: Some are scrolls that look almost new; many are scrolls yellowed with age.

You start looking through them and find that on some are descriptions of your life, of situations you are in, of your relationships; some of the writing goes back a long while, some is more recent. As you go through the scrolls, one by one, you begin to see that some describe situations you are currently in that do not feel good to you. Perhaps, as you sit there reflecting on this, you see that something in your life may have been harmful for quite a long while.

You know what to read next. You pick up a scroll, one particularly relevant, and look at it, read it. It describes a situation you are currently in and the more you read it, the better you understand the harm it may cause you if you allow the pattern to continue. So you read, then think, then read some more. At last, after serious reflection, you look up from the scrolls and see that next to you, there is a stick of red wax, a bronze stamp with the letter Tav, a candle in a dish, and some matches. They were there all along, but you have just noticed them. Now is the time to put an end to this matter, once and for all. So you pick up the pen, and you write at the bottom of the scroll you have been reading: "This must end." Then you sign it.

To a make this definite and irrevocable, you reach for the matches and light the candle. You fold the paper until you can no longer see the writing, heat the end of the sealing wax stick, and let the molten wax drip on the scroll. You pick up the stamp that says Tav and press it firmly into the wax, sealing the paper shut.

You feel Tav's energy coursing through you. The matter will end; this outcome is sealed and will not be reopened.

A Magic with Tav

This is not essential to make Tav magic work, but if it is possible for the person doing this magic to actually use sealing wax and a stamp (we own a set marked with Tav for performing the Working for others), then the energy from the physicality will be added and be of powerful help.

What is needed is sealing wax, a stamp with Tav on it for sealing the wax (but the stamp can be blank), a candle, and a piece of paper or parchment. The person the incantation is for may write something on the paper with mention of the situation they need to seal shut, but they don't have to. A few words will suffice, such as, "I will put a stop to this" or something to that effect. Just one word can be enough.

The lot Tav that belongs to the person the magic is for needs to be laid against their heart, if possible, while doing this. After writing the words, we fold the paper in three, making the third fold a little shorter so that the fold beneath it still shows. This is where the wax will go, sealing the words. Or one can put the paper in an envelope, instead. Heat the sealing wax over the candle and drip the hot wax on the closed flap. (Be careful with the flame and hot wax!) Then press the stamp on the wax to seal the paper or envelope shut. Accompany these actions with the words:

Ancestors Guardians
and all elohim

Rafael before me
Uriel behind me
Gabriel to my left
Uziel to my right

Give me the hot wax
and hand me the seal

Give me the power to
stamp all this shut.

Give me the hot wax
and hand me the seal

And thereby the power
to bring this to end.
Selah

Appendix

Examples of Lot Readings and Magic

Sample Lot Readings

A person came asking for lot casting, and the question she had was about a thorny relationship with a grown-up daughter that resulted in frequent altercations. What should she do about the constant bickering? When I cast lots for her, the reading was ר Resh, ת Tav, and ק Quf.

As you can see, the lots showed the beginning of the process (Resh) of putting a stop (Tav)—in other words, ceasing and desisting—to that constant bickering. Basically, the message was: Don't feed the negative energy by letting yourself be drawn into bickering. Be firm and simply stop this.

The last letter, Quf, also indicated that doing this was going to be very difficult in that it was going to cause her and possibly her daughter the monkey mind, which can show up when changes occur in one's pattern of behavior. Monkey mind is considered to be an almost unavoidable response when one is contemplating having to make difficult changes, so its occurrence in this casting was not a way of warning the querent off.

• • •

A man came in asking if he should try to repair his relationship with his wife or leave the marriage without explanations. The lots gave the following letters: א Aleph, פ Pe, and כ Kaf.

In this case, too, the casting was fairly down to earth and blunt. Aleph is the chieftain, Pe is the mouth, and Kaf is the blessing hand, so the meaning was pretty clear. Aleph says: Act as a chieftain (in other words, have some moral courage). Pe says: Speak up and speak out, speak your truth; that is, have a clear discussion with your wife rather than simply slinking away. Kaf means there is a blessing on this enterprise, so there was a possible chance of repairing the problem with some open dialogue.

• • •

A woman had found somebody willing to buy her house, which was all she owned after a nasty divorce from a gambling-addicted husband who had left her with nothing else. The potential buyer was a friend of her ex. Should she trust him?

The casting was: ר ל ע. Read from right to left: Resh, Lamed, Ayin. The interpretation was that she was at the beginning of a process of learning more about her options, such as legal and economic ones, before acting and that she needed to also go to the well of metaphysical soul knowledge to have more clarity to aid her in decision making.

Sample Lot Magic

Here are a couple of additional examples.

A Magic for Pregnancy and Birth

Let us say a pregnant woman is concerned with wanting to create the best circumstances for her pregnancy and birthing.

The purpose of the magic here would be to assist in bringing healthy outcomes for her and her baby. After the ritual permission has been given and the space prepared, we choose the lot for the magic.

We may choose the lot Samekh, for bliss, since we wish her a blissful pregnancy and birthing.

We hold the lot Samekh in our dominant hand with the image facing the woman. If we prefer, we can instead have the woman hold the lot so that she can see it all through the ritual. After reciting the lot poem for Samekh, we walk around her and focus on the blissful meaning of Samekh.

If we are holding the lot, we wave it gently over her as we go around her, as though we were smudging her with Samekh as amulet. If she is holding the lot, we can trace the letter in the air before us as we go. We circle her three times, gently calling or chanting the word "Samekh" or its lot poem to bring its energy in. Then we stop, face her, and say:

"May spirit as you understand it hear this: As the energy of Samekh enters your soul and your body and your heart, may its gentle power of serenity and bliss surround you and fill you. May your pregnancy and birthing of your child be a path of joy. May your ancestral mothers and their ancient mothers smile upon you and watch over you."

The we close to ritual by saying:

"The blessing/magic ritual is over. Go in peace."

We can change these closing words but not omit them, as we need to shut down the energy.

Some people ask whose lots to use in such ritual. The answer is: It doesn't matter. We can use our own lots or the lots of the person for whom the magic blessing ritual is being performed. Or both our lots and theirs. Or we can let them borrow ours.

As mentioned, we are not concerned in our tradition with others using our magical/ritual tools. Nothing, except our own bad intentions, can ever contaminate or sully them. We do, of course, believe in asking and being asked for permission to touch; and it is all right for either party to refuse.

A Ritual Healing for a Person Anxious about a Surgery

There are a variety of rituals for combating anxiety, which can focus either on alleviating the patient's fear or on achieving healing. The latter is the more common, so I will describe one of the rituals that helps promote healing.

Again, we ask for consent. When consent is given, we do the necessary preparations—anointing with perfumed oil or lighting incense or an imitation candle, setting intention, focusing on spirit with reverence.

We select a suitable lot—for example, Aleph, the chieftain, for calm strength—and explain this meaning to the person. If the person can stand, we stand in front of them for this. We hand them the lot to hold and ask them to open to its energy. We walk around them, first chanting the lot poem for Aleph, then toning the word Aleph while bringing the energy in. If they cannot stand and are lying down, we can hand them the lot, then slowly walk around their bed, chanting while they open to the energy. If walking around is not feasible due to space constraints, we just stand next to them and chant for about the length of time it would take to circle around them.

Then we take the lot from them and, in an outstretched hand and still chanting, pass the lot Aleph over their body, especially the hurt area. We do this *without* touching them, slowly passing our hand with the lot over their body at least two handspans away from their clothing and skin. The passes need to focus healing energy on the body part that needs the surgery. Then, we hand the lot back them to hold.

After any such ritual we say: *"The ritual is closed. The healing ceremony is done. The magic will stay with you for as long as you need it. We can now go our separate ways."*

This is one of the formulas lot casters use to shut down the magic space and return everything to this reality.

If we plan to see the person again socially, we wait at least ten or more minutes before resuming ordinary interaction.

These uses of Hebrew lots for divination, meditation, and magic can yield a rich spiritual harvest and benefit both lot caster and the recipient of the lots' bounty.

May the powers you revere smile upon you as you learn to use the lots and reap their rich harvest.

Glossary

Abraham, Abram: the names of the biblical patriarch. Both names refer to the same individual. Originally named Abram or Avram, the god eventually became Abraham (Avraham), meaning "father of many nations." Both names are used in this book, reflecting the one used at the time of reference.

AMHA: a reconstructionist Hebrew polytheist path with emphasis on earth, tribe, and ethics. The name derives from *Am Ha'aretz* and reclaims the phrase.

Am Ha'aretz: literally "people of the earth" or "man of the earth"; however, in a culture that prized scholarship, the term eventually developed derogatory overtones. By the 2nd century CE, it had come to mean "hayseed" or "ignoramus," indicating an uneducated person.

Ashera: the preeminent goddess of the Hebrew/Canaanite pantheon. She is a godform with various aspects: queen of the gods, mother goddess, and bringer of abundance. The name may be spelled in various ways. Ashera may refer to a personified godform, but may also refer to sacred pillars or trees. There are references in the Bible to the placing and removing of these Ashera figures from the Jerusalem Temple.

Ashera Tree: a sacred tree or pole that stood near Canaanite religious locations to honor the mother goddess Ashera.

Asherot: the plural form of Ashera, which may refer to a variety of female godforms.

Ayn Sof: a Hebrew term that is also transliterated into English as Ein Sof and which is literally translated as "without end." It refers to that which is infinite and unfathomable; a vast and pure high entity in its broadest, most transcendent form—so transcendent that it cannot be fully defined.

Baal: the monotheist redactors of the Bible left the impression that Baal was distinct from the Hebrew god. But they shared many characteristics, primarily those of a warrior god who leads the host (the army). Baal is not a proper name. It is a title that means husband, lord, owner, and master, even in today's modern Hebrew. As such, it could refer to a number of gods in the area as a title of respect.

Baalim: the plural form of Baal.

Bereshit: literally "in the beginning"; it is the first word of the Hebrew Bible and the title of its first book—the first of the Five Books of Moses. This book is titled Genesis in English.

B'nei Elohim: literally "children of the elohim" or "sons of the elohim"—the word may be interpreted either way—these are the junior godforms of the elohim. It is implied that the b'nei elohim are lower in rank than the elohim.

El: The father god of the Canaanite/Hebrew pantheon, as well as in some surrounding areas. His full name and title are El Elohim; that is, "god of (all) gods." Hebrew Bible redactors shortened it to Elohim. Historically, the name El appears to have been used in the northern areas of Israel; whereas in the south, the supreme god was typically called Yahweh. Eventually the two merged. When spelled with a lowercase "e," el may refer to any male god.

Elohim: the senior gods, godforms, or sacred powers of the Hebrew and Canaanite pantheons. The word is plural and spelled with a lowercase "e."

Kabbalist: a student, follower, or authority of the Jewish mystical tradition Kabbalah.

Minyan: a Hebrew word that refers to the quorum or minimum number of participants required for a ritual to take place. In Rabbinical Judaism, that number is ten, but AMHA and other spiritual traditions may have different requirements.

Selah: a mysterious Hebrew word that appears seventy-one times in the Psalms. It typically, although not exclusively, appears as a concluding word. The meaning of the word is now unknown; however, many believe it to be a musical direction.

Shophet: in the context of AMHA and this book, this refers to someone who is a leader, mediator, seer, and healer. The author of this book is a shophet.

Shophtim: plural form of the Hebrew word shophet.

Stela: an upright stone slab or column typically bearing a carved inscription or relief design, and which typically serves as either a commemoration or a gravestone.

Urim and Tumim: an element of the breastplate worn by the high priest, it served divinatory purposes.

Yaakov: the original pronunciation of the Hebrew name commonly spelled Jacob in English.

Recommended Reading

The following books offer some background to the topics in this book, but they are by no means the only ones. Some of the books cited are for scholars, others are intended for general readers, but all the authors are scholars of repute.

Cross, Frank Moore. *Canaanite Myth and Hebrew Epic: Essays in the History of the Religion of Israel.* Cambridge, MA: Harvard University Press, 1973.

Dever, William. *Who Were the Early Israelites and Where Did They Come From?* Grand Rapids: Wm. B. Eerdmans Publishing Co., 2003.

Friedman, Richard Elliott. *The Bible with Sources Revealed.* New York: HarperOne, 2005.

Friedman, Richard Elliott. *Who Wrote the Bible.* New York: Simon & Schuster, 1987.

Keel, Othmar, and Christoph Uehlinger. *Gods, Goddesses, and Images of God in Ancient Israel.* Minneapolis: Augsburg Fortress, 1998.

Patai, Raphael. *The Hebrew Goddess.* New York: Avon Books, 1978.

Schauss, Hayyim. *The Jewish Festivals: A Guide to Their History and Observance.* New York: Schocken Books, 1968.

Smith, Mark S. *The Origins of Biblical Monotheism: Israel's Polytheistic Background and the Ugaritic Texts.* New York: Oxford University Press, 2001.

Tailor, J. Glen. *Yahweh and the Sun: Biblical and Archaeological Evidence for Sun Worship in Ancient Israel.* Sheffield, UK: JSOT Press, 1993.

Walls, Neal H. *The Goddess Anat in Ugaritic Myth.* Atlanta: Society of Biblical Literature, 1991.

Zevit, Ziony. *The Religions of Ancient Israel: A Synthesis of Parallactic Approaches.* New York: Bloomsbury Academic, 2002.

About the Author

Elisheva Nesher, the elected leader of Am Ha Aretz (Primitive Hebrew Assembly), has been a spiritual teacher and mentor since the 1990s. A teacher, public speaker, and seer, she has served as a consultant to Pagan spirituality groups. Elisheva studied archaeology in Tel Aviv. A professional translator, she maintained a private psychotherapy practice until 2017.

To Our Readers

Weiser Books, an imprint of Red Wheel/Weiser, publishes books across the entire spectrum of occult, esoteric, speculative, and New Age subjects. Our mission is to publish quality books that will make a difference in people's lives without advocating any one particular path or field of study. We value the integrity, originality, and depth of knowledge of our authors.

Our readers are our most important resource, and we appreciate your input, suggestions, and ideas about what you would like to see published.

Visit our website at *www.redwheelweiser.com* to learn about our upcoming books and free downloads, and be sure to go to *www.redwheelweiser.com/newsletter* to sign up for newsletters and exclusive offers.

You can also contact us at *info@rwwbooks.com* or at

Red Wheel/Weiser, LLC
65 Parker Street, Suite 7
Newburyport, MA 01950